McDougal, Littell
SPELLING

Silver Level

Dolores Boylston Bohen
Language Arts Curriculum Specialist
Fairfax County, Virginia

Carolyn McConnell
Language Arts Teacher
Santa Barbara, California

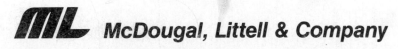 **McDougal, Littell & Company**

Evanston, Illinois
New York   Dallas   Sacramento   Raleigh

Objectives

- to teach the spelling of **words** as well as the spelling of sounds
- to stress the recognition of **structural** similarities as well as phonetic similarities
- to strengthen **associative** and **visual memory**
- to reinforce the **three modes of learning:** visual, auditory, and kinesthetic

Organization

Each lesson presents a word list that demonstrates one spelling pattern or generalization. The list is followed by three types of activities:

Practice the Words—three activities that require students to examine and write the words on the spelling list

Build Word Power—an activity that extends the application of words on the spelling list in a broader language arts context

Reach Out for New Words—two activities in which students work with new words that follow the spelling pattern

CONSULTANTS FOR THIS TEXT

Jan Abbott, Teacher, Flagstaff Unified School District 1, Flagstaff, Arizona
Margie Arcurie, Teacher, Kanawha County School District, Charleston, West Virginia
Carolyn Gross, Teacher, Denton Independent School District, Denton, Texas
Rose Harrison, Teacher, Lynchburg City School District, Lynchburg, Virginia
Sue Kampas, Teacher, Plano Independent School District, Plano, Texas
Julia Maxwell, Teacher, East Allen County School District, Fort Wayne, Indiana
Elaine Borim McGee, Clayton County School District, Jonesboro, Georgia

Acknowledgments
Random House, Inc.: For "September" from *A Child's Calendar* by John Updike; copyright © 1965 by John Updike & Nancy Burkert; reprinted by permission of Alfred A. Knopf, Inc. Viking Penguin, Inc.: For "Changing" from *Yellow Butter Purple Jelly Red Jam Black Bread* by Mary Ann Hoberman; copyright © 1981 by Mary Ann Hoberman.

ISBN: 0-8123-5321-8

Copyright © 1988 by McDougal, Littell & Company
Box 1667, Evanston, Illinois 60204
All rights reserved. Printed in the United States of America

88 89 90 / 15 14 13 12 11 10 9 8 7 6 5 4 3

Contents

A B C D E F G H I

J K L M N O P Q R

S T U V W X Y Z

a b c d e f g h i j

k l m n o p q r

s t u v w x y z

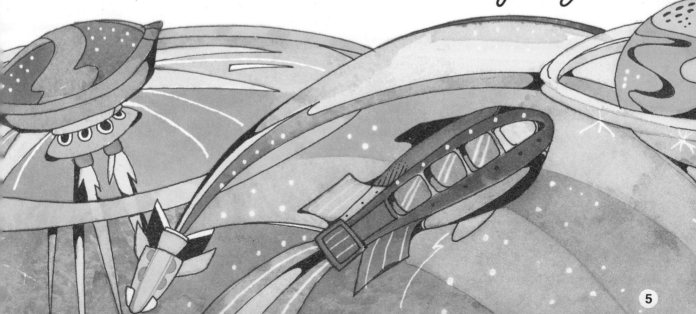

How To Spell a Word

Each week you will be learning to spell a new list of words. You will need a system for studying these words. Follow the steps below to master the spelling of a new word. You will find these steps helpful as you prepare for your weekly test.

1. Look at the new word.

2. Say the word.

3. Spell the word aloud.

4. Copy the word.

5. Picture the word in your mind.

6. Cover the word and write it.

   Check for mistakes. If you have made a mistake, repeat steps 1 through 6.

A Writer's Journal

Spelling Is for Writing

Imagine that you need to write a note telling your parents where you are going after school. What would happen if you could not spell any of the words needed for your message?

You learn to spell in order to write. You will use writing throughout your life to express your feelings and ideas. This book will help you improve both your spelling and your writing. The more you practice both skills, the better speller and writer you will become.

One fun way to practice writing is to keep a journal. A journal is a notebook in which you write about your thoughts and feelings. A journal is for your own use and enjoyment.

Plan to keep a journal throughout the year. Write in your journal often. On some days you might write only a sentence or two. On other days you might write several pages. Here are some ways to use your journal:

- tell about your feelings
- remember important events in your life
- describe something or someone of interest
- react to a poem or story you have read
- daydream on paper about anything that comes to your mind

Spelling and Your Journal

When you write, you may want to use words that you do not know how to spell. Do not stop writing. Write the words as you think they should be spelled. When you are finished, look up the correct spellings in the dictionary. Practice spelling these words using the method explained on page 6. Keep a list in the back of your journal of words that gave you trouble. You can refer to this list when you need to write the words in the future.

Getting Started

If you need an idea for your first journal entry, try one of these.

1. Today I've been thinking about . . .
2. I wish something unusual would happen.

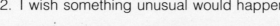

Final silent e words and suffixes

state	*stating*	*states*	*statement*
improve	*improving*	*improves*	*improvement*
measure	*measuring*	*measures*	*measurement*
amaze	*amazing*	*amazes*	*amazement*
divide	*dividing*	*divides*	
unite	*uniting*	*unites*	
practice	*practicing*	*practices*	
cause	*causing*	*causes*	
choose	*choosing*	*chooses*	

A **suffix** is a word ending that changes the use of a word.

1. The words in the first column end with a letter that cannot be heard. What is that silent letter?

2. When **ing** was added to the words in the first column, what happened to the final silent **e**?

3. When **s** and **ment** were added, what happened to the final silent **e**?

To add a suffix to a word that ends with a final silent **e**,
drop the **e** if the suffix begins with a vowel (**ing**).
Keep the **e** if the suffix begins with a consonant (**s**, **ment**).

A Write the final silent **e** words in alphabetical order. Cross out the final **e**. Then write the **ing** form of each word.

A **base word** is a word before any changes are made. A suffix can be added to a base word to change the way it is used.
John will <u>measure</u> the wall with a <u>measuring</u> tape and write down the <u>measurement</u>.
The underlined words are **related forms** of one word, **measure**.
Related forms of the same base word may be different parts of speech. They may be nouns, verbs, adjectives, or adverbs.

B Complete each pair of sentences with two different forms of the underlined word.

1. <u>choose</u>   Carlos always _____ the red bike.

_____ your birthday present was fun.

2. <u>measure</u>   We are _____ the windows for shades.

Which _____ was correct?

3. <u>unite</u>   A common goal _____ the team.

Our whole family is _____ for the holiday.

4. <u>state</u>   Mary is _____ her opinion.

Read the _____ at the top of the page.

5. <u>practice</u>   Sharon is _____ a difficult piece on the piano.

                     She _____ every day.

6. <u>divide</u>   Ken is _____ the cake evenly.

                     The fence _____ our two yards.

7. <u>cause</u>   Our class studied the two main _____ of the war.

                     What is _____ the problem?

8. <u>amaze</u>   Her face showed _____ when she read the note.

                     The trapeze artists did some _____ tricks.

9. <u>improve</u>   My math teacher said that my work was _____.

                     Some _____ is needed in our town's bus service.

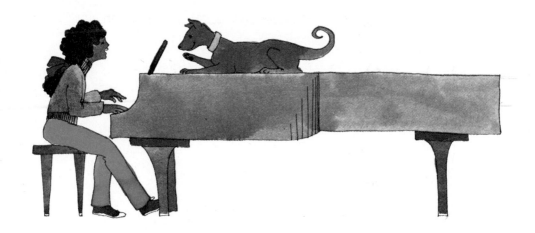

Proofreading

C Find the five misspelled words in the paragraph below. Write them correctly.

      Proofreading is an important skill to learn. It means training your eyes to catch mistakes in written work. After practiceing proofreading for a while, you will start seeing spelling mistakes everywhere. To your amazment, you will find them in newspaper statments, school notices, and store advertisements. Carelessness may be causeing a number of your own spelling mistakes. Greater awareness of misspellings will lead to improvment of your own writing.

stating	improvement	amazes	unites	choosing
states	measuring	amazement	practicing	chooses
statement	measures	dividing	practices	
improving	measurement	divides	causing	
improves	amazing	uniting	causes	

New Words
determine
starve
flame
retire
require
raise
separate
owe

Build Word Power

Writing

A **verb** is a word that tells about an action.
The verb ending **ed** shows that an action happened in the past.
It is an ending that begins with a vowel. When it is added to a word
that ends with silent **e**, drop the final **e**.

Drop the final **e** and add **ed** to each word below. Then answer the
questions using three of the **ed** words in complete sentences.

1. measure   **2.** cause   **3.** divide   **4.** improve   **5.** unite   **6.** practice

How did you share the last piece of pie?

How did you get ready to give your speech?

How did you know the size of the rug?

Reach Out for New Words

A The eight new silent **e** words with endings are hidden in two
directions in this puzzle. → ↓ Circle each word and write it.

```
r e t i r e m e n t y
e f b o r a i s e s t
q l c w a n e q u t e
u a s i g p n i d a s
i m q n k x l d f r o
r e l g b s r u n v m
e s s e p a r a t e d
d e t e r m i n e d f
```

B How many more related forms can you make by adding the endings **s,**
ed, ing, and **ment** to the new base words? Write the new forms on your own paper.

Lesson 2

The suffix **able**

break + able = *breakable*

reason + able = *reasonable*

suit + able = *suitable*

depend + able = *dependable*

read + able = *readable*

laugh + able = *laughable*

avail + able = *available*

allow + able = *allowable*

accept + able = *acceptable*

avoid + able = *avoidable*

wash + able = *washable*

wear + able = *wearable*

admire + able = *admirable*

use + able = *usable*

love + able = *lovable*

like + able = *likable*

move + able = *movable*

adore + able = *adorable*

1. The suffix **able** begins with a vowel that causes spelling problems because it is difficult to hear clearly or identify easily. What is this **indistinct** vowel?

2. How many of the words in the first column end with a silent **e**? When **able** is added to these words, what happens to the final **e**?

3. Do any of the other words change when **able** is added?

> The suffix **able** is commonly added to complete words to form adjectives meaning "able to be."   usable = able to be used
> The first letter of the **able** suffix cannot be clearly heard. The **a** is an indistinct vowel that may be mistaken for other vowels. When the suffix is added to complete words, it is usually spelled **able**, not **ible**.

Writing

A Answer each question with the **able** form of the spelling word. Begin each answer with the underlined words.

1. Can the old stove still be **used**?

2. Will these dishes **break**?

3. Does this room **suit** our needs?

4. Is the cost of the coat within **reason**?

5. Can you **read** the small print?

6. Do you **love** the new kitten?

7. Can you still **wear** the uniform?

8. Did you **laugh** at the old movie?

9. Can you **depend** on Chris?

10. Do you **like** the neighbors?

Mnemonics (Cover the silent first letter and say *ne mon'ics*)
Mnemonics is a system of improving the memory.
A mnemonic device is a memory aid.
For example, the word **HOMES** can help you to remember the names of the five Great Lakes.
Huron **O**ntario **M**ichigan **E**rie **S**uperior
Invent your own mnemonic devices for words that are spelling problems.

B Add the missing vowels to make spelling words. Write each word.

1. __ cc __ pt __ bl __

2. __ v __ __ d __ bl __

3. __ dm __ r __ bl __

4. __ v __ __ l __ bl __

5. __ ll __ w __ bl __

6. __ d __ r __ bl __

How many of the words begin with the letter **a**?
If you have trouble remembering how to spell the suffix in any of these six words, the first letter of the word can remind you of the first letter of the suffix:

   avoid**a**ble, not avoid**u**ble   **a**llow**a**ble, not allow**i**ble

You have just used a mnemonic device!

Dictionary

Guide words are the two words at the top of each dictionary page. They tell you the first word and the last word on the page.

Entry words are the words listed in alphabetical order in a dictionary. They are printed in dark type and divided into word parts called **syllables**.

The dictionary **entry** is the entry word and all the information that follows it.

C Alphabetize the spelling words that come between each pair of guide words.

1. accent/all   (3 words)
2. alligator/awake   (3 words)
3. bread/deposit   (2 words)
4. latitude/lilac   (2 words)

5. lounge/movie   (2 words)
6. reaction/reassure   (2 words)
7. urgent/weary   (3 words)

Build Word Power

Proofreading

The newspaper that printed these want ads had a careless proof-reader. Find the six misspelled words. Write them correctly.

For Sale

Admirable antique dresser, best offer
665-2215

Pictures suitible for framing, $2.00 each
668-2294

Sofa, still useble, $50.00
591-8820

Money problems? Help availeble. Booklet, Money Muscles, P.O. 250, Elridge, Virginia

Loveable puppy
Six months old. Free.
222-8179

Washible, wearable jackets. Write to Box W2 at this paper.

Moveable type, slightly used. 50¢ each.
778-1190

Trade-in allowable on new television
338-0042

breakable ✓ readable ✓ acceptable ✓ admirable ✓ movable ✓
reasonable ✓ laughable ✓ avoidable ✓ usable ✓ adorable ✓
suitable available washable lovable
dependable ✓ allowable ✓ wearable ✓ likable ✓

Reach Out for New Words

A Unscramble each group of letters to write a base word. Then add **able**
to each word. Watch out for base words with a final silent **e**.

1. nihsup ____ + able = ____

2. chare ____ + able = ____

3. vergiof ____ + able = ____

4. frotip ____ + able = ____

5. resiph ____ + able = ____

6. seerid ____ + able = ____

7. nafhiso ____ + able = ____

Writing

B Using one of your new **able** words, write a complete sentence that answers
each question. The underlined words will help you decide which word to use.

1. Did you make money from the garage sale?

2. Do bananas spoil easily?

3. Can a player be penalized for "stealing" second base?

4. Will the climbers be able to get to the top of the mountain?

5. Are last year's styles still popular?

6. Is "shooting" a picture a pardonable action?

7. Is sunny weather pleasing for a picnic?

15

Lesson 3

The suffix er/singular possessive

play + er =	*player*	*player's*
speak + er =	*speaker*	*speaker's*
report + er =	*reporter*	*reporter's*
travel + er =	*traveler*	*traveler's*
garden + er =	*gardener*	*gardener's*
lead + er =	*leader*	*leader's*
buy + er =	*buyer*	*buyer's*
build + er =	*builder*	*builder's*
paint + er =	*painter*	*painter's*
drive + er =	*driver*	*driver's*
manufacture + er =	*manufacturer*	*manufacturer's*
consume + er =	*consumer*	*consumer's*
advertise + er =	*advertiser*	*advertiser's*
announce + er =	*announcer*	*announcer's*
manage + er =	*manager*	*manager's*
purchase + er =	*purchaser*	*purchaser's*
produce + er =	*producer*	*producer's*
write + er =	*writer*	*writer's*

1. All of the words in the first column can be action words or _____ .
2. When **er** is added to the verbs in the first column, they become naming words or _____ .
3. How did the spelling of the last nine words change when **er** was added?
4. What has been added in the last column to make each singular noun show possession or ownership?

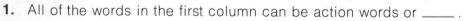

The suffix **er** is commonly added to verbs to make nouns that mean "one who does something."   speaker—one who speaks
Most singular nouns are made possessive by adding **'s**.

16

The plural and possessive forms of many nouns sound alike:
    players   player's
Most nouns are made plural by adding **s**.

A Write the **er** form of each verb below.

B Complete each sentence, using both the plural form and the singular possessive form of the **er** word.

play

   1. All the _____ cheered, but one _____ face was sad.

drive

   2. When the _____ returned, one _____ car was badly dented.

purchase

   3. Some _____ traded coupons at one
        _____ suggestion.

report

   4. _____ fought for the assignment, so the new _____ chances were slight.

announce

   5. Of all the _____ I have heard, I like that _____ voice best.

buy

   6. Dozens of _____ bid on the property before one _____ offer was accepted.

manufacture

   7. That _____ product is so well made that other _____ are trying to copy it.

travel

   8. The _____ enjoyed themselves until one _____ ticket was lost.

garden

   9. All the local _____ entered the flower show, but one _____ roses were sure to win.

manage

   10. One team _____ record was admired by all of the other _____.

lead

   11. When all the band _____ marched onto the field, our _____ baton could not be seen.

consume

   12. When the group of _____ met, each _____ problem was discussed.

advertise   **13.** One ____ clever commercials were envied by the other ____.

paint   **14.** The ____ were almost finished when one ____ bucket spilled.

build   **15.** One ____ houses had more room than those of the other ____.

produce   **16.** A group of movie ____ met to consider one ____ ideas.

Proofreading

C Apostrophe Annie sprinkles apostrophes everywhere and hopes that some of them land in the right place. Help Annie by proofreading this letter to her grandparents. Find the six plurals and possessives she has used incorrectly. Write them correctly.

Dear Grandma and Grandpa,

     I hope my two favorite traveler's are safely home now. I heard the radio announcer's forecast of bad storms when you left, but I know you are both careful driver's. Besides, weather reporter's are not always right!

     At our school assembly today, Steve won the best players trophy, and Michele won the band leader's award for the best musician. Some of the speaker's were a little nervous in front of all those people. I guess I would be, too.

     This is a short letter, but I have writers cramp from school today. I'll write another letter soon.

                 Love,
                 Annie

player's	gardener's	painter's	advertiser's	producer's
speaker	leader	driver	announcer	writer
reporter's	buyer's	manufacturer's	manager's	
traveler	builder	consumer	purchaser	

New Words

publish
examine
organize
labor
loaf
accuse

Build Word Power

Match one of the words below with a rhyming **er** word from your spelling list. Write each phrase.

 meeker

 fainter

 lighter

1. A softer talker is a _____.

2. A weaker artist is a _____.

3. A skinny author is a _____.

4. A little newsperson is a _____.

5. A taller customer is a _____.

 shorter

higher

Reach Out for New Words

A Look at the new **er** words above. Write the **er** word that means:

1. one who works hard

2. one who looks closely

3. one who complains against

4. one who puts things in order

5. one who seldom works

6. one who prints books

B Write the possessive form of each new **er** noun in a phrase. All the words in each phrase will begin with the same letter.

1. <u>a</u>wful <u>a</u>rgument

2. easy explanation

3. orderly operation

4. lazy look

5. long ladder

6. prize paperback

19

Prefixes and base words

re	+ new	=	*renew*
re	+ call	=	*recall*
re	+ fund	=	*refund*
re	+ move	=	*remove*
re	+ model	=	*remodel*
re	+ view	=	*review*
re	+ arrange	=	*rearrange*
re	+ form	=	*reform*
re	+ enter	=	*reenter*
re	+ invest	=	*reinvest*
re	+ fresh	=	*refresh*
de	+ frost	=	*defrost*
de	+ press	=	*depress*
de	+ code	=	*decode*
pre	+ historic	=	*prehistoric*
pre	+ view	=	*preview*
pre	+ position	=	*preposition*
pre	+ heat	=	*preheat*

A **prefix** is a group of letters attached to the beginning of a word to change its meaning.

1. What three prefixes have been added to complete words to make spelling words?

2. Does each prefix end with a vowel or a consonant?

3. When each prefix is added to a base word, does the spelling of the prefix change? Does the spelling of the base word change?

A prefix that ends with a vowel is added directly to a complete word to form a new word. No change is made in the prefix. No change is made in the base word.

Practice the Words

A Write the spelling word that completes each sentence.

1. Fossils of dinosaurs and other _____ animals were found in this cave.

2. Always _____ your spelling words before a test.

3. Will the store _____ our money?

4. Do you _____ the name of Pam's street?

5. Nothing will _____ the paint stain from the rug.

6. The word **of** is an example of a _____.

7. Will the chicken _____ in time for dinner?

8. You will not be able to _____ the room without a key.

9. Our neighbors plan to _____ their house this summer.

10. News of the pitcher's injury will certainly _____ the fans.

11. The committee will try to _____ those poor working conditions.

12. The secret agent tried to _____ the message.

B Find the misspelled word in each group. Write it correctly.

1. refform	2. preview	3. refund	4. rennew	5. reenvest
depress	recall	rearange	review	reenter
prehistoric	rimove	defrost	preposition	remodel

6. preview	7. recall	8. prehistoric	9. preheat
rearrange	remove	rimodel	decode
prepposition	preeview	depress	rafresh

Dictionary

Prefixes are listed in the dictionary as separate entries. Each entry may give several meanings for a prefix.

C Read the entries for the prefixes **re**, **pre**, and **de** in your spelling dictionary. Write the meanings. Then write the spelling words that match the definitions.

1. press *down*
2. look at *again*
3. look at *before*
4. invest *again*
5. call *back*
6. heat *before*

7. take *away* frost
8. set up *again*
9. give *back* money
10. make new *again*
11. come in *again*
12. *before* written history

Build Word Power

Writing

Read this acrostic poem and answer the questions.

Remember the day
Each of us
Came to school
And we
Lost our
Lunch boxes?

What spelling word is made with the first letter of each line? How is the meaning of that word related to the idea in the poem?

Write acrostic poems with two of your spelling words.

22

renew   remodel   reenter   depress   preposition
recall   review   reinvest   decode   preheat
refund   rearrange refresh   prehistoric
remove   reform   defrost   preview

New Words
Discover
new words
below!

Reach Out for New Words

A Build a word pyramid by following
the code. Write each new word.

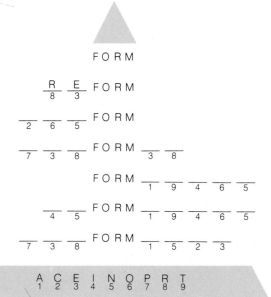

FORM

$\underset{8}{R}\ \underset{3}{E}$ FORM

$\underset{2}{\quad}\ \underset{6}{\quad}\ \underset{5}{\quad}$ FORM

$\underset{7}{\quad}\ \underset{3}{\quad}\ \underset{8}{\quad}$ FORM $\underset{3}{\quad}\ \underset{8}{\quad}$

FORM $\underset{1}{\quad}\ \underset{9}{\quad}\ \underset{4}{\quad}\ \underset{6}{\quad}\ \underset{5}{\quad}$

$\underset{4}{\quad}\ \underset{5}{\quad}$ FORM $\underset{1}{\quad}\ \underset{9}{\quad}\ \underset{4}{\quad}\ \underset{6}{\quad}\ \underset{5}{\quad}$

$\underset{7}{\quad}\ \underset{3}{\quad}\ \underset{8}{\quad}$ FORM $\underset{1}{\quad}\ \underset{5}{\quad}\ \underset{2}{\quad}\ \underset{3}{\quad}$

$\underset{1}{A}\ \underset{2}{C}\ \underset{3}{E}\ \underset{4}{I}\ \underset{5}{N}\ \underset{6}{O}\ \underset{7}{P}\ \underset{8}{R}\ \underset{9}{T}$

B Build another word pyramid. Find
the last four words in your spelling
dictionary and write the definitions.

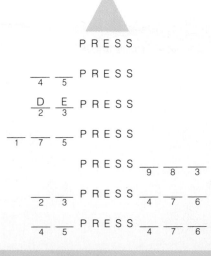

PRESS

$\underset{4}{\quad}\ \underset{5}{\quad}$ PRESS

$\underset{2}{D}\ \underset{3}{E}$ PRESS

$\underset{1}{\quad}\ \underset{7}{\quad}\ \underset{5}{\quad}$ PRESS

PRESS $\underset{9}{\quad}\ \underset{8}{\quad}\ \underset{3}{\quad}$

$\underset{2}{\quad}\ \underset{3}{\quad}$ PRESS $\underset{4}{\quad}\ \underset{7}{\quad}\ \underset{6}{\quad}$

$\underset{4}{\quad}\ \underset{5}{\quad}$ PRESS $\underset{4}{\quad}\ \underset{7}{\quad}\ \underset{6}{\quad}$

$\underset{1}{C}\ \underset{2}{D}\ \underset{3}{E}\ \underset{4}{I}\ \underset{5}{M}\ \underset{6}{N}\ \underset{7}{O}\ \underset{8}{R}\ \underset{9}{U}$

Prefixes and roots

re	+ spond	=	*respond*
re	+ flect	=	*reflect*
re	+ peat	=	*repeat*
re	+ sult	=	*result*
re	+ spect	=	*respect*
re	+ vise	=	*revise*
re	+ duce	=	*reduce*
re	+ sume	=	*resume*
de	+ posit	=	*deposit*
de	+ cide	=	*decide*
de	+ tach	=	*detach*
de	+ flate	=	*deflate*
de	+ tect	=	*detect*
pre	+ vent	=	*prevent*
pre	+ tend	=	*pretend*
pre	+ judice	=	*prejudice*
pre	+ dict	=	*predict*
pre	+ cise	=	*precise*

Roots are word parts that cannot stand alone. They grow into words when
they are joined to prefixes (added before roots) or suffixes (added after roots).

1. Before the prefixes **re**, **de**, and **pre** are added in the first column,
   are the letter groups complete base words?

2. A word part that must be joined to a prefix or suffix to make a
   complete word is called a _____ .

3. When the prefixes and roots are joined, does the spelling
   of either word part change?

A prefix that ends with a vowel can be added directly to roots to
form words. The spelling of the prefix does not change. The
spelling of the root does not change.

Practice the Words

A Complete each sentence with a spelling word.

1. Did anyone _____ to Kerry's letter?

2. Give the carpenter the _____ measurements of the room.

3. The ranger told us how to _____ forest fires.

4. Did you _____ what you want for lunch?

5. Remember to _____ your papers before you hand them in.

6. The lawyer tried to _____ the jury against the defendant.

7. Dale went to the bank to _____ his money.

8. The store will _____ the price of bathing suits in August.

9. The coach will _____ all the basketballs before she stores them.

10. The forecaster did not _____ rain for the weekend.

11. Someone should _____ the trailer from the car.

12. What was the _____ of the experiment?

13. We should always show _____ for the beliefs of others.

14. Did you only _____ to be sleeping?

15. The lake can _____ images like a blue mirror.

B Write the **ed** and **ing** forms of spelling words. If a spelling word ends with a final silent **e**, drop the **e** before writing the other forms.

1. reflect

2. result

3. respect

4. revise

5. reduce

6. detect

7. deflate

8. pretend

9. deposit

10. decide

25

Dictionary

Most dictionary entries are base words. Other forms of the word may be included within the base word entry.

re·duce (ri dōōs′) *v.* **1** to make smaller, less, fewer, etc.: decrease [to *reduce* taxes: to *reduce* speed]. **2** to lose weight, as by dieting. —**re·duced′, re·duc′ ing**

word forms shown

Word forms are usually *not* included in the base word entry unless the spelling of the base word changes when the endings are added.

re·spect (ri spekt′) *v.* **1** to feel or show honor for [We *respect* learned people.] **2** to be thoughtful about [to *respect* others' rights]. ◆*n.* a feeling of honor or polite regard [He has great *respect* for his father.]

no word forms shown

C Look at these word forms. First write the entry word you would look up to find the meaning of each word form. Then tell whether the word form would be found in the base word entry.

1. responded
2. prejudicing
3. revised
4. prevented
5. repeating
6. detached
7. predicting
8. resumed
9. detecting

Build Word Power

Write the spelling word that matches each definition. Then find the word in the definition that gives the meaning of the prefix.

1. to give back an image *reflect*

2. to begin again

3. to say again

4. to tell about something before it happens

5. to undo one thing from another

6. to send back an answer

7. to stop something before it happens

8. to take air away from

respond   respect   deposit   detect   predict
reflect   revise   decide   prevent precise
repeat   reduce   detach   pretend
result   resume   deflate   prejudice

New Words
Discover
new words
below!

Reach Out for New Words

A Build a word pyramid by following the code. Use your spelling dictionary to find the four pyramid words that match the definitions.

| The root **duc** means "lead." |

1. someone who leads an orchestra

2. "lead" people to know each other

3. to "lead away from" or make less

4. ceremony that leads people into a club

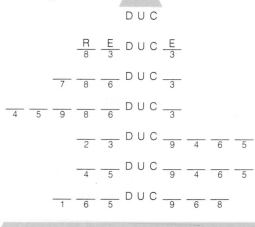

B Build another word pyramid. Use your spelling dictionary to find four pyramid words that match the definitions.

| The root **dic** means "speak." |

1. speak before or ahead of time

2. that which is spoken against

3. one whose word is law

4. final word or truth

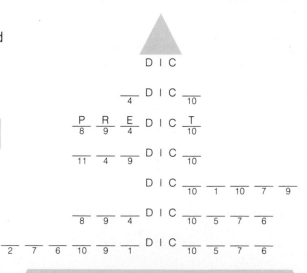

Plurals formed with es

bus + es = *buses*

campus + es = *campuses*

recess + es = *recesses*

guess + es = *guesses*

address + es = *addresses*

business + es = *businesses*

leash + es = *leashes*

crash + es = *crashes*

couch + es = *couches*

porch + es = *porches*

sandwich + es = *sandwiches*

speech + es = *speeches*

wristwatch + es = *wristwatches*

waltz + es = *waltzes*

tax + es = *taxes*

prefix + es = *prefixes*

suffix + es = *suffixes*

mailbox + es = *mailboxes*

1. How many words in the first column end with the letter **s**?
2. How many end with **sh**?   with **ch**?
3. How many end with **x**?   with **z**?

When a word ends with **s**, **sh**, **ch**, **x**, or **z**, add **es** to make the plural form.

Practice the Words

A Complete each phrase with a spelling word.

1. four yellow school _____

2. visited several college _____

3. wrote their names and _____

4. a house with front and back _____

5. two ten-minute _____ each day

6. danced several _____

7. added different _____ to the end of the word **journey**

8. wore _____ to know the time

9. runs two successful _____

10. added different _____ to the beginning of the word **place**

11. saw two minor car _____

12. kept the dogs on _____

13. listened to a few short _____

14. pillows for the _____

15. _____ in front of the post office

16. ate two _____

B Find the plural forms of ten of your spelling words that will fit in the puzzle.

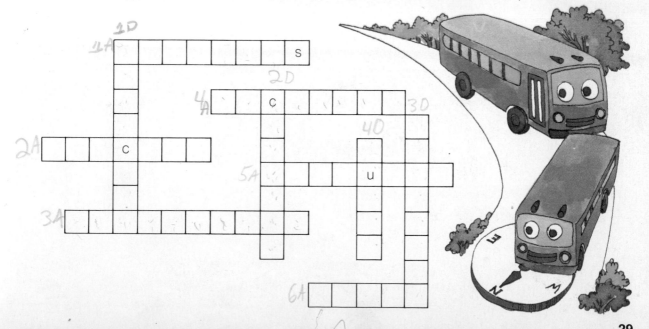

Dictionary

A dictionary entry tells the different uses and meanings of a word. Parts of speech are abbreviated. Different meanings are numbered. Some meanings are illustrated with a sample sentence or phrase.

part of speech — **tax** (taks) *n.* money one pays to support the government •*v.* **1** to put a tax on [Congress has the power to *tax* the people.] **2** to put a burden or strain on. — numbered definitions — sample sentence

C Find one spelling word that can be used as more than one part of speech in each pair of sentences. Write the sentences. Then look up that word in your spelling dictionary. Beside each sentence, write the abbreviation for the part of speech of the word as it is used in the sentence. If there is more than one definition, also write the number of the meaning that fits the sentence.

1. Write the _____ on the envelopes. _____
   Marge _____ the envelopes carefully. _____

2. Fifty years ago, _____ were popular dances. _____
   No one _____ as gracefully as my grandparents. _____

3. We paid out _____ last month. _____
   Mountain climbing _____ my strength. _____

4. You get three _____ to solve the riddle. _____
   Robbie always _____ the right answers. _____

5. Two plane _____ occurred last week. _____
   The damaged tower _____ to the ground. _____

6. Our class has two _____ every day. _____
   Congress _____ at the end of the year. _____

Build Word Power

Writing

On your own paper, write concrete poems with two or more of your spelling words. Make a shape with each word that reminds you of its meaning.

buses	addresses	couches	wristwatches	suffixes
campuses	businesses	porches	waltzes	mailboxes
recesses	leashes	sandwiches	taxes	
guesses	crashes	speeches	prefixes	

New Words
aroh
climax
duplex
flash
rash
search
sinus
walrus
wrench

Reach Out for New Words

A Find the correct path through the maze. Words that add **es** to make the plural form are on the right path. Write the nine words that are on your path.

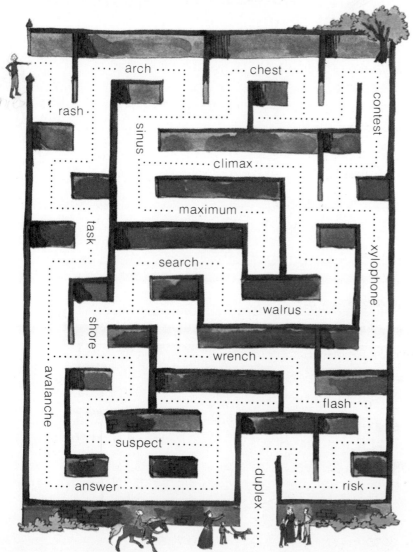

B Write the plural form of the nine new words.

Lesson 7

Soft and hard g

gigantic

giant	guest
register	regulate
magic	magazine
margin	magnet
average	against
strange	slogan
surgery	sugar
angel	angle

gorgeous

1. Look at the words in the first column.
   What vowels come after the letter **g** in these words?
   Does the letter **g** have a soft sound (<u>gi</u>n<u>g</u>er) or a hard sound (<u>g</u>um)?

2. Look at the words in the second column.
   What letters come after the letter **g**?
   Does the letter **g** have a hard or a soft sound?

3. Look at the words **gigantic** and **gorgeous**.
   Which **g** in **gigantic** is hard? Why?
   Which **g** in **gorgeous** is soft? Why?

> When the letter **g** has a soft sound, it is usually followed by the
>   letters **i** or **e**.
> When the letter **g** has a hard sound, it is usually followed by a
>   consonant or by the vowels **a**, **o**, or **u**.

A Complete each of the list words below by adding the missing letters.

Soft **G** Words	Hard **G** Words
__ __ __ __ __ GE	GU __ __ __
GI __ __ __	__ __ __ GA __
__ __ GE __	__ GA __ __ __ __
__ __ __ GI __	__ GA __ __ __
__ __ __ __ GE	__ __ GN __ __
__ __ GE __ __	__ __ GL __
__ __ GI __	__ __ GU __ __ __
__ __ GI __ __ __ __	__ __ GA __

GIGA __ __ __ __

GORGE __ __ __

The last two words contain both the hard and the soft sounds of the
letter **g**.

B Complete each phrase with a spelling word.

1. a heavenly ____
2. read a ____
3. ____ at a hotel
4. a weekend ____
5. ____ the thermostat
6. about ____ height
7. big as a ____
8. an entertaining ____ show

9. a ninety-degree ____
10. cream and ____
11. reasons for and ____
12. recovering from ____
13. a ____ redwood tree
14. the pull of the ____
15. an advertising ____
16. the right ____ of the page

Proofreading

C Proofread the following sentences. Find the misspelled words.
Rewrite the sentences, correcting the errors.

1. The averag person was frightened by the gentle gaint simply
   because he was giantic.

2. The huge manget attracted metal like magac.

3. The magazine offered strang prizes for the most original slogen
   mailed to the editor.

4. Contestants could register by mailing the coupon found in the
   bottom margun.

5. The painting looks gorgous aganst the white wall.

Build Word Power

The letters of each of these words are contained in one or more of your
spelling words. Write one of those spelling words. Then write another
hard **g** word made from some of the letters of the same spelling word.

1. goal _slogan_ _gas_

2. gear

3. grant

4. gate

5. greet

34

gigantic margin angel magnet angle
giant average guest against gorgeous
register strange regulate slogan
magic surgery magazine sugar

New Words

guitar	figure
fragile	guard
refrigerator	regiment
passenger	propaganda

Reach Out for New Words

A Use each set of clues to find a new word with a soft or hard **g**. Write each word.

1. Provides protection; rhymes with **hard**

2. Plays music; has three vowels

3. Rides a bus; sounds like **messenger**

4. Keeps food cold; sounds like **waiter**

5. A number; begins with a fruit

6. Breaks easily; has four consonants

7. Group of soldiers; rhymes with **tent**

8. Can persuade; has four syllables

B Choose three of the new words. Use the letters in each word to make as many other words with a hard or soft **g** as you can.

35

1

improve	improving	improvement
measure	measuring	measurement
practice	practicing	practices
choose	choosing	chooses

Pick one

2

reason	reasonable
use	usable
like	likable

3

gardener	gardener's
leader	leader's
writer	writer's
builder	builder's

4

model	remodel
arrange	rearrange
view	preview

5

revise
deflate
decide

6

address	addresses
business	businesses
speech	speeches
bus	buses

7

giant
magazine
angle
average

Using Review Words

A An analogy is a special way of showing how words go together. Look at the first pair of words in each row. In what way do these words go together? Write a spelling word that makes the second pair of words go together in the same way.

1. **notice** is to **noticing** as **revise** is to _____

2. **address** is to **addresses** as **business** is to _____

3. **owe** is to **owing** as **practice** is to _____

4. **love** is to **lovable** as **like** is to _____

5. **improve** is to **improvement** as **measure** is to _____

6. **new** is to **renew** as **model** is to _____

7. **arch** is to **arches** as **speech** is to _____

8. **play** is to **player's** as **write** is to _____

9. **preview** is to **previewed** as **decide** is to _____

10. **enter** is to **reenter** as **arrange** is to _____

B Complete these sentences with spelling words.

1. Have you written the _____ on the envelopes?

2. The _____ was ten inches taller than an _____ person.

3. Tom read the _____ from cover to cover.

4. Are those old school _____ still _____?

5. The _____ landscaping bill was very _____.

6. Did you _____ to watch the _____ of the new show?

7. My pitch is _____ now that I'm _____ every day.

8. Use a compass to measure each _____ of the triangle.

9. Will the puncture cause the balloon to _____?

10. The band members followed their _____ directions.

C One word in each group is misspelled. Find the misspelled word and write it correctly.

1. measurement
   useable
   preview
   speeches

2. magazine
   practicing
   addresses
   leder

3. likable
   revise
   choseing
   prejudice

4. buses
   bilder
   remodel
   average

5. angle
   writer
   decide
   gaint

6. reasonable
   rearrange
   improvment
   businesses

Using More Review Words

A Use the directions following each word to make another form of the word.

1. strange   add **er**

2. announce   add **ment**

3. report   add **er**

4. unite   add **re**

5. decide   add **ing**

6. remove   add **able**

7. regulate   add **tion**

8. remove   add **er**

9. consume   add **able**

10. advertise   add **ing**

11. rearrange   add **ment**

12. write   add **ing**

13. use   add **ing**

14. manage   add **ment**

15. respect   add **able**

B Three words in each row follow the same spelling pattern. One word does not. Write that word. Be ready to tell why it does not belong.

1. slogan   choose   angle   magnet

2. readable   address   suitable   laughable

3. respond   renew   reflect   respect

4. waltzes   leashes   guesses   statement

5. announcer   manager   margin   painter

6. average   strange   magic   prehistoric

7. reduce   defrost   remove   depress

8. taxes   buses   causes   porches

C Look at the first pair of words in each row. In what way do the words go together? Find a word in the box that makes the second pair of words go together in the same way. Complete the analogy by writing that word.

reduce	gardeners	magnet	predict	reflect
respond	producer	average	deposit	laughable

1. **visitor** is to **guest** as **ordinary** is to _____

2. **subtract** is to **add** as **withdraw** is to _____

3. **more** is to **increase** as **less** is to _____

4. **magazine** is to **readable** as **joke** is to _____

5. **depart** is to **leave** as **maker** is to _____

6. **past** is to **remember** as **future** is to _____

7. **magnet** is to **attract** as **mirror** is to _____

8. **melt** is to **defrost** as **answer** is to _____

9. **bee** is to **honey** as **metal** is to _____

10. **potatoes** are to **farmers** as **roses** are to _____

group	members	held	everyone
taken	parents	cue	anywhere
acted	makeup	eyes	setting
hardly	putting	role	clothes
tale	center	cost	handling

Prewriting. Prewriting is the thinking and planning you do before you begin to write. Thinking about your ideas helps you to decide what you want to write. Making prewriting notes helps you to plan and organize your ideas. In this lesson you will plan and write a **paragraph that tells what happened**.

Use Prewriting Skills

A Answer these questions with spelling words. The words will help you think about the details of a school play.

1. What word means "the story the play tells"? What word means "the part the actor plays"?

2. What may be put on an actor's face? What part of the face does a good actor use well?

3. What word is a hint for an actor to move or speak?

4. What is another name for the scenery on the stage?

5. What word names the middle of the stage?

6. What four words could refer to people who might help with or attend a play?

7. What five verbs could be used to describe actions connected with a play?

8. What is a simple name for costumes?

9. What word might refer to the price of tickets?

10. What two adverbs could complete this sentence to describe a crowded theater? There was ＿＿ a seat ＿＿ in the auditorium.

B To plan a paragraph well, write down your ideas. You will notice that many of your notes tell about one particular idea. This can be the main idea of your paragraph.

Here are some prewriting notes that Scott wrote about getting ready for a play.

everyone was given a role   cast members learned lines
chose play about a fairy tale   practiced acting on cue
will choose serious play next   enjoyed putting on clothes and makeup for
director helped run tryouts   dress rehearsal
                                           held cast party after second show

Scott looked over his notes. Here's what he decided his main idea should be:

It took weeks of work to get our play ready for opening night.

Not all of Scott's notes fit that idea. Find those that do not belong. Then write the six notes that do tell about Scott's main idea.

C The ideas in a paragraph must be in an order that makes sense. When you write a paragraph that tells a story, put the ideas in the order in which they happened.

Look at the prewriting notes you wrote for Exercise B. Number them in an order that makes sense.

Now Think

Plan your own paragraph about a show you saw or were in. Think about all the things that had to be done to get ready for the show. Who made the costumes and scenery? Did everyone learn the lines? Think about opening night. Did any funny or scary things happen?
Now follow these prewriting steps:
1. Choose your topic.
2. Make a list of ideas about your topic.
3. Read your notes to see how they fit together.
4. Decide on a main idea for your topic.
5. Cross out ideas that don't belong.
6. Number the rest in an order that makes sense.

Writing. Your first try at putting ideas into sentence and paragraph form is called a **first draft**. Begin with a topic sentence that tells the main idea. Then write other sentences to add details about what happened.

Your details should be clear and interesting. Sometimes you can combine two sentences to make your details clearer.

> **Example:** The actor suddenly moved. *He moved* from the center of the stage.
> The actor suddenly moved from the center of the stage.

The new sentence tells the same idea as the two sentences. Only the important words were used. The words in italics were left out.

Use Writing Skills

Combine the sentences in each pair. Add the important words from the second sentence. Decide which words to leave out.

1. Daily practice had been held. It had been held at school.

2. Helpers were setting up chairs. The chairs were in the gym.

3. We exchanged our clothes for the costumes. The costumes were on the rack.

4. All the cast members wore makeup. They wore it on their faces and around their eyes.

5. Handling the scenery was difficult. The scenery was heavy.

6. Parents took group pictures. They took them after the curtain call.

Now Write   Look at your prewriting notes. Use them to write a first draft of your paragraph about a show. Begin with a strong topic sentence that tells what the paragraph is about. Add details in the order that they happened. Try to write interesting sentences that do not repeat unnecessary words.

Revising. When you revise your first draft, you make changes to improve your writing. First revise your ideas. Then proofread carefully to find mistakes in grammar, capitalization, punctuation, and spelling.

One important part of revising is checking to see that you have chosen exact or specific words. Notice the differences between these two sentences.

> The beggar, dressed in <u>old</u> clothes, <u>walked</u> across the stage.
> The beggar, dressed in <u>tattered</u> clothes, <u>hobbled</u> across the stage.

Use Revising Skills

A Rewrite the following sentences on your own paper. Replace general words with the more specific words in parentheses.

1. Tom acted the role of the king and spoke orders to his men.
(bellowed, knights)
2. Mary was dressed as a dog and ran onto the center of the stage.
(bounded, poodle)
3. Ms. Nelson was fixing our clothes and helped us with putting on our makeup.
(adjusting, smoothing)
4. Tony sat on his big hat and couldn't find another anywhere.
(sombrero, squashed)
5. The cast members were glad when everyone in the audience expressed approval.
(thrilled, applauded)

B Proofread this first part of a paragraph about a play. Mark all the mistakes in capitalization, punctuation, and spelling. Then rewrite the paragraph correctly on your own paper.

Remember • Indent the first line of a paragraph.
• Begin every sentence with a capital letter.
• End every sentence with the correct end mark.

On opening night we learned that practice doesn't always make us perfect. first two cast members missed their cues. They caused us to leave out a whole scene? Our stage manager accidentally closed the curtain. The ropes stuck and we could hardly get it open we also had trouble handleing the scenery we forgot to move the old seting from center stage. We were amazed when everyone clapped at the end.

C Revise the following first draft. Then rewrite it correctly on your own paper. The directions below will help you.

1. Find one sentence that is not about the main idea.
2. Combine two sentences in lines 6 and 7.
3. Replace two underlined words with more lively language.
4. Find the six misspelled words. Write them correctly.
5. Correct the capitalization errors in lines 3, 5, 6, and 9.
6. Correct the punctuation error in line 7.

1   This year's play about pioneers was one of our best shows

2   ever! Everone in the class had a roll to play. Tom acted the part of

3   columbus and <u>looked</u> out from behind a cardboard Santa Maria. Tom's sister

4   said the tickets cost too much. Then several membres of our group

5   dressed as Pilgrims and acted out the first thanksgiving. They were

6   followed by a covered wagon. it was pulled on cue by four boys. The boys

7   were pretending to be pioneers? Next onto center stage <u>came</u> children

8   dressed as pioneers in medicine, industry, and science. Last of all were

9   the Astronauts. Their spaceship was supposed to be takin up into the

10   loft by the crew. Unfortunately, the girls handling the pulley couldn't get it to

11   move anywhare. Our ship didn't make it to the stars, but each actor in

12   the tail was a star in the eyes of the parents!

Now Revise

Read the first draft of your own story about a show. Does each sentence tell about the main idea? Are your sentences in an order that makes sense? Have you used lively language? Do you need to combine any sentences? Remember to proofread for mistakes in grammar, capitalization, punctuation, and spelling.

Make a neat copy of your paragraph. You will want to share it with others. Show your friends how the process of writing has helped you produce a paragraph you can be proud of.

A Writer's Journal

In her book *How I Came To Be a Writer,* Phyllis Reynolds Naylor shares her thoughts and experiences as a writer. In the paragraph in the box she tells one of the things a person must do to become a good writer. Read the paragraph. Then discuss the questions with the class.

1. Why does the author say that the place to begin writing "is obviously yourself"?

2. Imagine that you are about to write a story about a five-year-old boy or girl. What would be a good way to decide how the boy or girl will feel or act?

> Writing means remembering how you felt when you were small, being aware of how you feel right now, and speculating on how you will feel when you are old. It is a combination of real feelings and experiences all mixed up with imaginings, and the place to begin is obviously yourself.
>
> —PHYLLIS REYNOLDS NAYLOR

Now use the paragraph as a starting point for your next journal entry. Here are some ideas to use.

1. Tell about one of your earliest memories. Try to describe the memory using as many senses as possible: sight, sound, smell, taste, and touch.

2. Invent a character for a story. Write a description of how the character looks, feels, and acts. Model the character after yourself.

3. Tell what you will be like when you are 70 years old. Include such things as how you will look, what your likes and dislikes will be, and how you will spend most of your time. Use your imagination.

Spelling and Your Journal

Sometimes when you are writing, you want to use a word that you do not know how to spell. If this happens, follow these steps.

1. Continue writing. Write the word as you think it should be spelled.

2. After you have finished writing, check to see if the word is on the list at the back of your journal. If not, look up the word in the dictionary.

3. Correct your spelling and add the word to your list.

4. Practice spelling the word several times.

LINIC

45

Lesson 10

Final y words and suffixes

✓ delay	*delays*	*delayed*	*delaying*
✓ enjoy	*enjoys*	*enjoyed*	*enjoying*
✓ destroy	*destroys*	*destroyed*	*destroying*
✓ journey	*journeys*		
✓ alley	*alleys*		
✓ satisfy	*satisfies*	*satisfied*	*satisfying*
identify	*identifies*	*identified*	*identifying*
✓ rely	*relies*	*relied*	*relying*
✓ enemy	*enemies*		
✓ diary	*diaries*		

1. What is the last letter of each word in the first column?
2. How many words have a vowel before the final letter?
3. When the letter before the final **y** is a vowel, what happens to the **y** when a suffix is added?
4. When the letter before the final **y** is a consonant, what happens to the **y** when the suffix **es** or **ed** is added?
5. When the suffix **ing** is added to any final **y** word, what happens to the letter **y**?

When the letter before a final **y** is a vowel, the **y** does not change when a suffix is added.
When the letter before the final **y** is a consonant, change the **y** to **i** before adding **es** or **ed**.
Never change the **y** to **i** when adding the suffix **ing**.

Practice the Words

Most nouns are made plural by adding **s** or **es**.

A Rewrite each sentence, changing the underlined nouns to the plural form. Find one other spelling word in each sentence.

1. Did you enjoy your <u>journey</u> to the city?

2. A fire in the attic destroyed the old <u>diary</u>.

3. Delivery trucks in the <u>alley</u> can delay other cars.

4. The army relies on radar to locate its <u>enemy</u>.

The **ed** ending is added to verbs to show that an action happened in the past.

B Complete each sentence with the **ed**, or **past tense**, form of six verbs from your spelling list.

1. We ____ our trip until next week.

2. The old house was ____ by the fire.

3. We ____ on our guide to lead us.

4. Everyone ____ the carnival.

5. The buyer was not completely ____ with the purchase.

6. The detective never ____ the mysterious stranger.

C Alphabetize the spelling words that come between each pair of guide words. Write the form of the word that would be the entry word in a dictionary.

1. hysterics / king   (2 words)
2. relax / suppose   (2 words)
3. enact / enlarge   (2 words)
4. degree / diet   (3 words)
5. act / comet   (1 word)

Build Word Power

Words that have almost the same meaning are called **synonyms**.
Words that have opposite meanings are called **antonyms**.

Write the spelling word that is either an antonym or synonym of each word. The two words should have the same word ending.

1. depending   (synonym)   *relying*
2. hurried   (antonym)
3. friends   (antonym)
4. trips   (synonym)
5. passages   (synonym)
6. discontented (antonym)
7. named   (synonym)
8. disliked   (antonym)
9. journals   (synonym)
10. constructs   (antonym)

delays   enjoying   alloyc ✓   identified ✓   enemies ✓
delayed ✓   destroys ✓   satisfies   identifying   diaries ✓
delaying   destroyed   satisfied   relies
enjoys ✓   destroying   satisfying   relied
enjoyed   journeys ✓   identifies   relying

New Words

omploy   medley
injury   terrify
beauty   apology
luxury

Reach Out for New Words

A Write the **s** or **es** forms of the seven new words that fit in this puzzle.

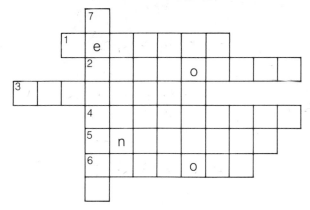

B Use this code to find eight more related forms that follow the final **y** pattern. Write each word.

Q	S	V	K	G	C	M	A	D	O	B	W	I
1	2	3	4	5	6	7	8	9	10	11	12	13

L	R	E	U	Y	F	Z	P	T	H	X	J	N
14	15	16	17	18	19	20	21	22	23	24	25	26

1. 13   26   25   17   15   16   9

2. 22   16   15   15   13   19   13   16   9

3. 14   17   24   17   15   13   10   17   2

4. 8   21   10   14   10   5   13   20   16

5. 11   16   8   17   22   13   19   17   14

6. 16   7   21   14   10   18   13   26   5

7. 13   26   25   17   15   13   10   17   2

8. 22   16   15   15   13   19   18   13   26   5

49

The suffix ly

personal + ly = *personally*

ideal + ly = *ideally*

original + ly = *originally*

mental + ly = *mentally*

annual + ly = *annually*

final + ly = *finally*

legal + ly = *legally*

actual + ly = *actually*

real + ly = *really*

fatal + ly = *fatally*

equal + ly = *equally*

normal + ly = *normally*

local + ly = *locally*

punctual + ly = *punctually*

individual + ly = *individually*

artificial + ly = *artificially*

total + ly = *totally*

continual + ly = *continually*

1. All of the words in the first column can be used as adjectives. They all end with the letters _____.
   These words are changed to adverbs by adding the suffix _____.
2. What are the last four letters of each word in the last column?
3. When the suffix **ly** was added, did the spelling of the base word or the suffix change?

> Add the suffix **ly** directly to adjectives ending with **al**.
> Do not drop the **l** at the end of the base word. Do not drop the **l** in the **ly** suffix.
> **Mnemonic device:** Don't lose **Al**!   person-**al**-ly
> Pronounce each syllable.

Practice the Words

A Make a spelling word with each group of scrambled syllables. There is one extra syllable in each group.

1. gal on ly le
2. gal ly qual e
3. tal fin men ly
4. lo tal ly fa
5. al re de ly
6. cal le ly lo
7. ly mal men nor
8. tal un ly to
9. al tin u con ly re

10. son al nal per ly
11. punc ly nu al an
12. rig al o in ly an
13. tu ly ac al an
14. ly tu punc an al
15. al de i ly ul
16. nal ly fi al
17. dev al in u vid ly di
18. cial ar me ti ly fi

B Write the spelling word that fits each shape.

1.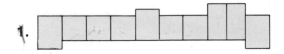
2.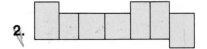
3.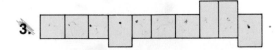
4.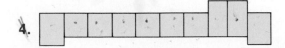
5.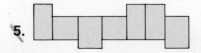
6.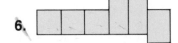
7.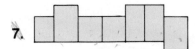
8.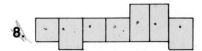
9.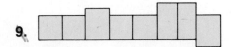
10.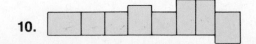

51

Dictionary

Suffixes may be listed as entries in a dictionary.	**—ly** (lē) *a suffix used to form adjectives and adverbs, meaning:* **1** of, like, or suitable to [*Friendly* advice is advice like that a friend would give.] **2** every or each [A *weekly* newspaper appears every week.]
Words formed by adding suffixes may also be entries.	**lo·cal·ly** (lō′k'l ē) *adv.* within a particular place [The storm did much damage *locally*.]
Other words with suffixes may be found at the end of a base word entry. Each of these words is followed by an abbreviation that tells the part of speech.	**punc·tu·al** (pungk′choo wəl) *adj.* coming, or doing something, at the right time; prompt. **—punc′tu·al′·i·ty** *n.* **—punc′tu·al·ly** *adv.*

C Make two columns on your paper and label them as shown below. Find each **ly** spelling word in your dictionary. Each word may be listed as a separate entry or at the end of an entry. Write it under the correct heading.

Separate Entry (12 words)   **End of Entry** (6 words)

Build Word Power

Writing

Change each underlined adjective in the first phrase to an adverb that will fit in the second phrase. Do this by adding the **ly** suffix. Then expand the second phrase to a sentence.

1. <u>local</u> farm   = ____ grown tomatoes

2. <u>equal</u> shares   = ____ divided the pie

3. <u>original</u> plan   = ____ planned to go

4. <u>final</u> decision = ____ decided to stay

personally annually really locally totally
ideally finally fatally punctually continually
originally legally equally individually
mentally actually normally artificially

New Words	
nation	fact
accident	nature
alphabet	crime

Reach Out for New Words

A Make other **ly** adverbs by following each set of directions.
   Start with a noun.
   Add a suffix to make the noun into an adjective.
   Add **ly** to the adjective to form an adverb.

1. Start with the word **nation**.
      Add **al** for a _____ leader.
      Then add **ly** for a _____ known leader.

2. Start with the noun **accident**.
      Add **al** for an _____ discovery.
      Then add **ly** for _____ discovered the cure.

3. Start with the noun **alphabet**.
      Add **ical** for _____ order.
      Then add **ly** for _____ listed.

4. Start with the noun **fact**.
      Add **ual** for a _____ report.
      Then add **ly** for a _____ written report.

5. Start with the noun **nature** (final silent **e** word).
      Add **al** for _____ flavor.
      Then add **ly** for _____ flavored ice cream.

6. Start with the noun **crime** (silent **e** word).
      Add **inal** for a _____ act.
      Then add **ly** for a _____ serious offense.

Writing

B Use five of your new **al** or **al + ly** words to write a story. Pretend you are a reporter. You are sent to a strange nation to investigate a terrible crime. Someone has stolen the alphabet!

53

The suffix ous

humor + ous = *humorous*

mountain + ous = *mountainous*

danger + ous = *dangerous*

marvel + ous = *marvelous*

glamor + ous = *glamorous*

poison + ous = *poisonous*

hazard + ous = *hazardous*

adventure + ous = *adventurous*

ridicule + ous = *ridiculous*

fame + ous = *famous*

nerve + ous = *nervous*

monotone + ous = *monotonous*

joy + ous = *joyous*

glory + ous = *glorious*

study + ous = *studious*

fury + ous = *furious*

victory + ous = *victorious*

vary + ous = *various*

1. How many of the words in the first column end with a silent **e**?
   What happened to the final **e** when **ous** was added?
2. How many words in the first column end with a **y**?
   How many of them changed the **y** to **i** when **ous** was added?
   Why didn't the final **y** change in one word?
3. Did the spelling of the other words change when the **ous** suffix was added?

The **ous** suffix is added to complete words to make adjectives
meaning "full of" or "having certain characteristics":
poisonous = full of poison   famous = having fame

Practice the Words

A Add the missing vowels to each word. Write the word.

1. m ___ ___ nt ___ ___ n ___ ___ s

2. m ___ rv ___ l ___ ___ s

3. p ___ ___ s ___ n ___ ___ s

4. f ___ m ___ ___ s

5. v ___ r ___ ___ ___ s

6. gl ___ m ___ r ___ ___ s

7. r ___ d ___ c ___ l ___ ___ s

8. v ___ ct ___ r ___ ___ ___ s

9. h ___ m ___ r ___ ___ s

10. d ___ ng ___ r ___ ___ s

11. j ___ y ___ ___ s

12. ___ dv ___ nt ___ r ___ ___ s

13. n ___ rv ___ ___ s

14. gl ___ r ___ ___ ___ s

15. h ___ z ___ rd ___ ___ s

16. f ___ r ___ ___ ___ s

17. m ___ n ___ t ___ n ___ ___ s

18. st ___ d ___ ___ ___ s

B The underlined word in each phrase is an antonym for a spelling word.
Substitute the spelling word with the opposite meaning. Write each phrase.

1. flat land

2. defeated army

3. unhappy event

4. safe trip

5. terrible show

6. unknown author

7. serious story

8. calm driver

Proofreading

C Proofread this TV schedule for ten misspelled words. Write the misspelled words correctly.

Monday

CH	6:00
2	Humorus Happenings with Agatha Yakker
4	Adventureous Archie
9	Ridiculus Cartoon Capers
11	Victorious Victor

CH	7:00
2	Exercise with Furyous Fred
4	The Case of the Poisonos Pen
9	Game Show—Marvelous Money Madness
11	Health—Joious Jogging

CH	8:00
2	1962 Movie-Dangerous Journey
4	Various Sports
9	Galmorious Stars of Yesteryear
11	The Nerveous Nautilus

CH	8:30
4	Safety Special—Hazerdous Household Habits
9	Travelogue—Our Mountainous Northwest
11	Fameous Follies of 1920

Build Word Power

Writing

Write a phrase with each pair of words. Use the **ous** form of both words. Add **ly** to one of the **ous** words.

1. study / monotone
2. victory / glory
3. danger / adventure
4. humor / nerve
5. glamor / marvel

humorous	glamorous	ridiculous	joyous	victorious
mountainous	poisonous	famous	glorious	various
dangerous	hazardous	nervous	studious	
marvelous	adventurous	monotonous	furious	

New Words

melody
villain
luxury
traitor
vigor
prosper

Reach Out for New Words

A Find six new **ous** words by following this code. Each letter in a word is represented by a capital letter and a number.

C2 = v

	A	B	C	D	E	F	G
1	i	u	m	i	o	a	o
2	i	r	v	r	s	e	a
3	u	v	i	s	u	o	s
4	o	u	d	o	i	t	u
5	n	g	t	i	o	u	o
6	t	u	l	l	s	l	x
7	l	p	r	o	u	r	s

1. C2 E4 C6 F6 G2 A1 A5 E1 E7 D3
2. B3 A1 B5 E1 D2 F3 B1 G7
3. C1 F2 A7 G1 C4 D1 E5 A3 E2
4. F4 B2 F1 C3 A6 G5 D2 A4 B6 G3
5. D6 B4 G6 E3 C7 A2 F3 B6 D3
6. B7 C7 D4 E6 B7 F2 D2 D7 A3 D3

B Write the base word, the **ous** form, and the **ly** form of each new word.

57

Negative prefixes

un + necessary	=	*unnecessary*
un + numbered	=	*unnumbered*
un + named	=	*unnamed*
un + successful	=	*unsuccessful*
un + identified	=	*unidentified*
dis + respectful	=	*disrespectful*
dis + satisfied	=	*dissatisfied*
dis + trust	=	*distrust*
dis + agree	=	*disagree*
dis + appear	=	*disappear*
in + convenient	=	*inconvenient*
in + capable	=	*incapable*
in + considerate	=	*inconsiderate*
in + dependent	=	*independent*
mis + fortune	=	*misfortune*
mis + judge	=	*misjudge*
mis + placed	=	*misplaced*
mis + count	=	*miscount*

1. Is the last letter of each prefix a vowel or a consonant?
2. Are any letters added or dropped when
   the prefixes are added to the base words?
3. How does the prefix change the meaning of each word?

> Add the prefixes **un**, **dis**, **in**, and **mis** to base words without
>   changing any letters. When the last letter of the prefix is the
>   same as the first letter of the base word, *keep both letters*:
> >   di**ss**atisfied   u**nn**ecessary
>
> A word formed by adding one of these negative prefixes will mean
>   the opposite of the base word.

Practice the Words

Writing

A Write a complete answer to each question using a spelling word. Begin each answer with the underlined phrase from the question.

Example: How dependent is the new nation?
The new nation is independent.

1. Was Susan's answer respectful?
2. Has the burglar been identified?
3. Was the customer satisfied?
4. Is it necessary to have note paper?
5. Have they chosen a name for the new baby?
6. Was the team successful?
7. Are the arithmetic problems numbered?
8. Can those players judge distance accurately?
9. Do Kevin's parents agree with him?
10. Is that location convenient for you?
11. Did the lucky charm bring him good fortune?
12. Were his actions considerate?
13. Where did you place the keys?
14. Is he capable of carrying it alone?
15. Will the magician make the coins appear?
16. Do some people trust their first impressions?

B Unscramble the letters to make spelling words. First find the prefix, which is not scrambled. Then write each word.

1. dietnifunied
2. gradisee
3. penindendet
4. enoinnvcteni
5. tadefiidisss
6. tonumisc

7. plamisedc
8. dujmisge
9. fnumistore
10. brunneedmu
11. streedisplufc
12. turtsdis

C Complete each analogy with a spelling word. Some analogies are based on synonyms. Some are based on antonyms.

1. **busy** is to **idle** as **needed** is to _____
2. **punctual** is to **tardy** as **victorious** is to _____
3. **humorous** is to **funny** as **unable** is to _____
4. **build** is to **destroy** as **thoughtful** is to _____
5. **soundless** is to **silent** as **nameless** is to _____
6. **destroy** is to **ruin** as **vanish** is to _____

Build Word Power

Write the base form of each spelling word. Then write the base word with the new suffix.

1. unnamed _____ + ly = _____
2. unidentified _____ + able = _____
3. unnumbered _____ + ing = _____
4. disrespectful _____ + able = _____
5. independent _____ + able = _____
6. disagree _____ + able = _____
7. dissatisfied _____ + ing = _____
8. unnecessary _____ + ly = _____
9. misplaced _____ + ment = _____
10. misjudge _____ + ing = _____

unnecessary unnamed disagree inconsiderate misplaced
unnumbered disappear disrespectful independent misjudge
unidentified dissatisfied inconvenient misfortune
unsuccessful distrust incapable miscount

New Words
Discover new words below!

Reach Out for New Words

A Build a word pyramid by following the code. Use your spelling dictionary to find the four pyramid words that match the definitions.

> The root **pend** means "hang."

1. the hanging part of a grandfather clock

2. jewelry that hangs on a chain

3. "hanging" on someone or something

4. not "hanging" on anything else

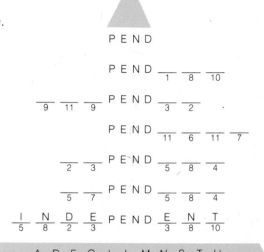

PEND

PEND __ __ __
      1 8 10

__ __ __ PEND __ __
9 11 9   3 2

PEND __ __ __ __
     11 6 11 7

__ __ PEND __ __ __
2 3   5 8 4

__ __ PEND __ __ __
5 7   5 8 4

I N D E PEND E N T
5 8 2 3   3 8 10

A D E G I L M N S T U
1 2 3 4 5 6 7 8 9 10 11

B Build another word pyramid. Use your spelling dictionary to find the four pyramid words that match the definitions.

> The root **cess** means "go" or "move."

1. a method of going from one step to another

2. a desired outcome; "moved" up to a goal

3. go away from work for a time

4. not needed

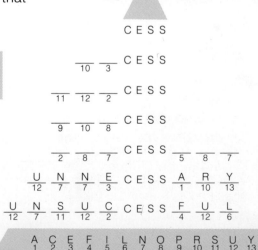

CESS

__ __ CESS
10 3

__ __ __ CESS
11 12 2

__ __ __ CESS
9 10 8

__ __ __ CESS __ __ __
2 8 7   5 8 7

U N N E CESS A R Y
12 7 7 3   1 10 13

U N S U C CESS F U L
12 7 11 12 2   4 12 6

A C E F I L N O P R S U Y
1 2 3 4 5 6 7 8 9 10 11 12 13

More prefixes and roots

con + tain	=	*contain*
con + tact	=	*contact* ✓
con + duct	=	*conduct* ✓
con + tent	=	*content*
con + vict	=	*convict* ✓
ex + port	=	*export* ✓
ex + cept	=	*except* ✓
ex + plore	=	*explore* ✓
ex + tend	=	*extend* ✓
in + tend	=	*intend* ✓
in + spect	=	*inspect* ✓
in + vite	=	*invite* ✓
in + ject	=	*inject* ✓
in + scription	=	*inscription*
sub + ject	=	*subject* ✓
sub + scription	=	*subscription* ✓
sub + tract	=	*subtract* ✓
sub + scribe	=	*subscribe* ✓

1. What are the four prefixes added to make spelling words?

2. Are the prefixes joined to complete words or to roots?

3. Do **extend** and **intend** have the same root?
   Do they have the same meaning?

4. Do **subject** and **inject** have the same root?
   Do they have the same meaning?

Words can be formed by joining prefixes and roots. A root can be combined with many different prefixes. Changing the prefix changes the meaning.

Practice the Words

A Write a spelling word to complete each phrase. Use each word only once.

1. the _____ of the sentence
2. to _____ the orchestra
3. a _____ to my favorite magazine
4. all _____ for one person
5. to _____ the penicillin
6. to _____ the time limit by five minutes
7. to _____ the mysterious old house
8. to _____ eighteen from thirty
9. _____ to dinner

10. my _____ lens
11. the _____ on the plaque
12. to _____ farm products to other countries
13. _____ to finish tomorrow
14. to _____ the flooded area
15. to _____ three quarts of water
16. to _____ someone of a crime
17. _____ to the daily newspaper

B Complete these analogies. The first two words will be either synonyms or antonyms. Write the spelling word that will make the same relationship between the next two words.

1. **awake** is to **asleep** as **add** is to _____
2. **leave** is to **depart** as **hold** is to _____
3. **come** is to **go** as **import** is to _____
4. **help** is to **assist** as **topic** is to _____
5. **talk** is to **speak** as **stretch** is to _____

63

Dictionary

C Find the prefixes **con**, **sub**, **ex**, and **in** in your spelling dictionary. Write the meaning or meanings given in the dictionary entry. Write the spelling words that use each prefix.

1. con (5 words)

2. sub (4 words)

3. ex (4 words)

4. in (5 words)

Build Word Power

Dictionary

Four spelling words can change their pronunciations as well as their meanings. Decide which word belongs in each pair of sentences. Then divide the words into syllables. Mark the accents to show how the pronunciation of the word changes. Finally, write the abbreviation for the part of speech of each word. Use your dictionary to help you.

1. A guide will _conduct_ us on a tour of the museum. _con·duct′ v._

 The teacher praised Lon's ____ in school.

2. The ____ will spend several years in prison.

 Did the jury ____ the defendant of a crime?

3. Which ____ do you have before math?

 We had to ____ our dog to a series of injections.

4. A sleeping cat always looks so ____.

 The ____ of this book is hard to understand.

64

contain   convict   extend   inject   subtract

contact   export   intend   inscription   subscribe

conduct ✓   except   inspect   subject ✓

content ✓   explore   invite   subscription

New Words
Discover
new words
below!

Reach Out for New Words

A Build a word pyramid by following the code. Use your spelling dictionary to find the four pyramid words that match the definitions.

> The root **scrib** means "write."

1. write your name on a magazine order

2. write carelessly

3. write about something

4. write in metal or marble

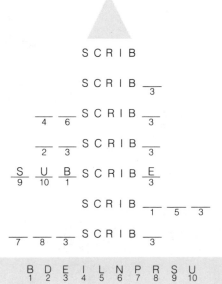

S C R I B

S C R I B __
3

__ __ S C R I B __
4   6   3

__ __ S C R I B __
2   3   3

S U B S C R I B E
9 10 1   3

S C R I B __ __ __
1   5   3

__ __ __ S C R I B __
7   8   3   3

B D E I L N P R S U
1 2 3 4 5 6 7 8 9 10

B Build another word pyramid. Use your spelling dictionary to find the four pyramid words that match the definitions.

> The root **spec** means "look."

1. a person who looks on or watches

2. to look upon as guilty

3. look closely to evaluate

4. event that causes everyone to look

S P E C

I N S P E C T
5 7   11

__ __ S P E C __
10 12   11

__ __ S P E C __ __ __ __
5   7   11 5 8 7

S P E C __ __ __ __ __
11 1 11 8 9

S P E C __ __ __ __ __
11 1 3 6 4

__ __ S P E C __ __ __ __ __
9   4   11 1 2 6 4

A B C E I L N O R S T U
1 2 3 4 5 6 7 8 9 10 11 12

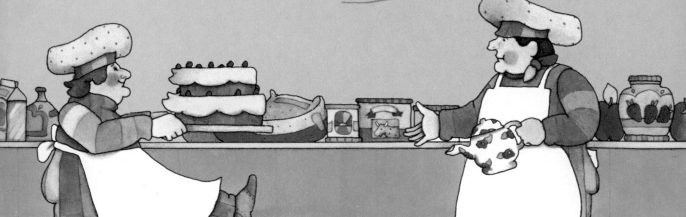

discovery   scenery
delivery   machinery
grocery   nursery
pottery   slavery
bakery   bravery
flattery   drapery
robbery   refinery
misery   mystery
      celery
      cemetery

1. What are the last three letters of each word?
2. When the final **y** is removed from the first eight words, complete words remain. What are the last two letters of those words?
3. When the **ry** is removed from the next seven words, complete words remain. What is the last letter of those words?

The suffix **ery** is a noun ending. An **ery** noun often contains a base word that ends with a final silent **e** or with **er**.

66

Practice the Words

A Complete each sentence with a spelling word.

1. A baby might sleep in a _____.

2. An artist might paint _____.

3. An explorer might make a _____.

4. A mail carrier might make a _____.

5. A hero might act with _____.

6. A ceramic shop might sell _____.

7. A fabric shop might sell _____.

8. A tyrant might practice _____.

9. A mechanic might work with _____.

10. A thief might commit a _____.

11. Vegetables might be sold in a _____.

12. Anyone might enjoy hearing some _____.

13. Oil might be processed in a _____.

14. Pastry might be sold in a _____.

15. A toothache might cause _____.

16. A farmer might grow _____.

17. A quiet place might be a _____.

18. A detective might solve a _____.

B Each word is part of a spelling word. Write the spelling word.

1. chin

2. cover

3. rap

4. liver

5. rave

6. is

7. fin

8. met

Write the four words that contain the word **very**.

Proofreading

C Proofread the ads in this shopping center directory. Write the ten misspelled words correctly.

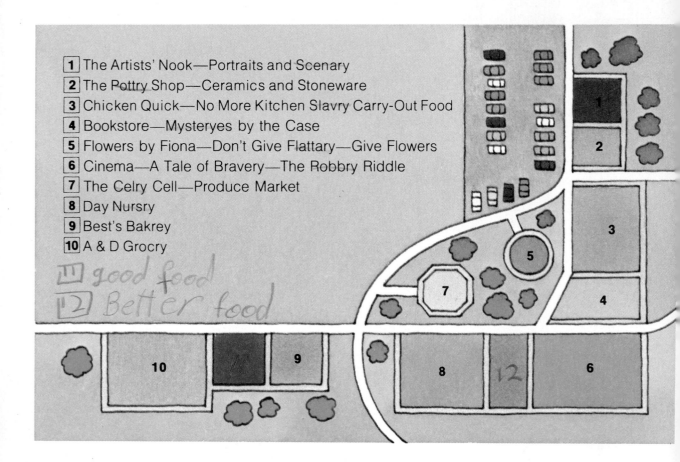

1 The Artists' Nook—Portraits and Scenary
2 The Pottry Shop—Ceramics and Stoneware
3 Chicken Quick—No More Kitchen Slavry Carry-Out Food
4 Bookstore—Mysteryes by the Case
5 Flowers by Fiona—Don't Give Flattary—Give Flowers
6 Cinema—A Tale of Bravery—The Robbry Riddle
7 The Celry Cell—Produce Market
8 Day Nursry
9 Best's Bakrey
10 A & D Grocry

[1] good food
[2] Better food

Build Word Power

Find the verb within each spelling word. Then add the suffixes **s**, **ed**, and **ing** to make three other verb forms.

1. discovery
2. bakery
3. delivery
4. flattery
5. refinery

discovery   bakery   scenery   bravery   celery
delivery   flattery   machinery   drapery   cemetery
grocery   robbery   nursery   refinery
pottery   misery   slavery   mystery

New Words
Discover
new words
below!

Reach Out for New Words

A Find six new **ery** words by following the code. Each letter in a word is represented by a capital letter and a number.

	A	B	C	D	E	F	G	H
1	t	e	r	e	r	y	r	e
2	e	m	k	c	m	s	t	i
3	l	t	a	e	n	i	t	y
4	e	r	o	t	c	l	e	g
5	r	o	p	c	y	e	c	r
6	e	o	y	r	n	a	o	y
7	s	l	y	y	h	t	y	p
8	y	k	r	k	r	e	a	e

1. B2   C4   E3   F6   A7   G3   H1   H5   D7
2. H4   C3   F4   A3   H8   C1   E5
3. F2   D4   G8   B3   H2   B6   E6   A2   G1   H6
4. A7   A3   F3   C5   H7   A4   E8   A8
5. F7   B4   F3   G5   C2   D3   E1   H3
6. E4   B5   G6   B8   A6   D6   C7

Writing

B Write sentences using four of your new words. Use the plural form of two words. Some of the words do not have a plural form. Look in your spelling dictionary to be certain.

The silent h

chemical
chorus
chrome
chlorine
chord
school
ache
echo
schedule
orchestra
architecture
anchor
mechanic
stomach
rhyme
rhythm
rhinoceros
rhubarb

1. In how many words does the silent **h** come after the letter **c**?
2. What one letter does the **ch** sound like in these words?
3. What letter comes before the silent **h** in the other words?

The letter **h** hides in many words without making a sound of its own. It is often silent in the combinations **ch** and **rh**.

A Complete the sentences with spelling words.

1. My _____ was upset after my third hot dog.
2. Dan plays the trumpet in our school _____.
3. We clapped to the _____ of the drums.
4. The ship dropped its _____ during the storm.
5. Many ruins show the beauty of early Greek _____.
6. A dangerous _____ polluted the water.
7. The _____ is repairing Uncle Joe's car.
8. Did your leg muscles _____ after the long hike?
9. Do you have a copy of the bus _____?
10. We heard his voice _____ across the valley.
11. Our new car has shiny _____ hubcaps.
12. Holly likes me to read her favorite nursery _____.
13. Our _____ colors are blue and white.
14. Ashley said the _____ was the most wrinkled animal at the zoo.
15. The _____ of a song is usually repeated.
16. We cooked the _____ from our garden.
17. Can you play this _____ on the piano?
18. The water in the swimming pool contains _____.

B Complete each analogy. The words are related in several different ways.

1. **kite** is to **sight** as **dime** is to _____
2. **brake** is to **car** as _____ is to **boat**
3. **plumber** is to **pipes** as _____ is to **motors**
4. **air** is to **lungs** as **food** is to _____
5. **oak** is to **wood** as _____ is to **metal**
6. **argument** is to **quarrel** as _____ is to **pain**
7. **kennel** is to **dog** as **zoo** is to _____
8. **water** is to **liquid** as **DDT** is to _____

C Use the clues to complete the word puzzle. Line up the words as shown below. Then find the hidden word that stretches from the top to the bottom of the puzzle.

1. a plant used as food

2. a chemical used in swimming pools

3. group of musical notes

4. list of times and places

5. DDT

6. musical beat

7. sound coming back

8. place to learn

9. digestive organ

10. singing group

11. group of musicians

12. person who repairs motors

1. _ _ _ _ _ _ _
2. _ _ _ _ _ _ _
    3. _ _ _ _ _
    4. _ _ _ _ _ _ _ _
5. _ _ _ _ _ _ _
  6. _ _ _ _ _ _
      7. _ _ _ _ _
    8. _ _ _ _ _ _
    9. _ _ _ _ _ _
10. _ _ _ _ _
    11. _ _ _ _ _ _ _ _ _
    12. _ _ _ _ _ _ _

Hidden word: _____

Build Word Power

Writing

Write acrostic poems with two of your spelling words. Each line begins with a letter of the word. The poem should tell something about the word.

Echo
Each voice is
Clearly
Heard
Over the valley.

Ache
An awful
Crash
Hurt my
Elbow

chemical ✓   chord ✓   schedule ✓   mechanic ✓   rhinoceros
chorus ✓   school ✓   orchestra   stomach ✓   rhubarb ✓
chrome   ache ✓   architecture rhyme
chlorine   echo ✓   anchor ✓   rhythm ✓

Reach Out for New Words

A Find eight new silent **h** words. The word **ache** has already been found for you. Find your way out of the maze. Write each word.

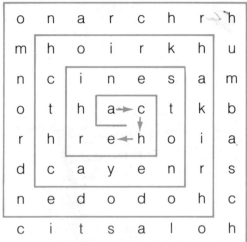

ache

o	n	a	r	c	h	r	h
m	h	o	i	r	k	h	u
n	c	i	n	e	s	a	m
o	t	h	a → c	t	k	b
r	h	r	e ← h	o	i	a
d	c	a	y	e	n	r	s
n	e	d	o	d	o	h	c
c	i	t	s	a	l	o	h

B Write the new word that matches each clue. Use your spelling dictionary to help you.

1. You could sail on it.

2. You could sing in it.

3. You could obey one.

4. You could wear clothes made of it.

5. You could have jewelry made of it.

6. You could grow bushes of it.

7. You could use it instead of **academic**.

8. You could dance it.

10

enjoy	enjoys	enjoyed	enjoying
satisfy	satisfies	satisfied	satisfying
rely	relies	relied	relying
diary	diaries		

11

final	finally
real	really
equal	equally

12

fame	famous
nerve	nervous
study	studious

13

successful	unsuccessful
necessary	unnecessary
dependent	independent
judge	misjudge

14

except
contain
invite
subscription

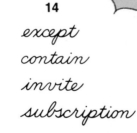

15

discovery
grocery
scenery

16

schedule
stomach
rhyme
rhythm

74

Using Review Words

A Complete each analogy with the correct form of a spelling word.

1. **fortune** is to **misfortune** as **judge** is to _____

2. **identify** is to **identified** as **satisfy** is to _____

3. **inject** is to **subject** as **inscription** is to _____

4. **baker** is to **bakery** as **grocer** is to _____

5. **ideally** is to **ideal** as **finally** is to _____

6. **enemy** is to **diary** as **enemies** is to _____

7. **glory** is to **glorious** as **study** is to _____

8. **inconsiderate** is to **consider** as **independent** is to _____

9. **nervous** is to **nerve** as **famous** is to _____

10. **inexcusable** is to **excusable** as **unsuccessful** is to _____

11. **numbered** is to **unnumbered** as **necessary** is to _____

12. **satisfy** is to **satisfying** as **rely** is to _____

Proofreading

B Proofread the paragraph for eight misspelled words. Write each word correctly.

Holly was realy nerveous about planning the surprise party for Cristina. She was careful not to give her friend a hint. Cristina asked Holly why she was being so mysterious. Holly tried to contane her smile and explain that she was just busy lately. Cristina seemed satisfied. Holly enjoied keeping the secret. Finaly, when the day of the party arrived, Holly made a terrible discovry. She had remembered to invit everyone exsept Cristina!

C Each underlined word is in the wrong phrase. Change the words around so the phrases make sense. Write each phrase correctly.

1. beautiful mountain <u>rhyme</u>
2. arrived on <u>rhythm</u>
3. the <u>stomach</u> of the drums
4. <u>scenery</u> shared the work
5. had an upset <u>grocery</u>
6. a nursery <u>equally</u>
7. shopped at the <u>schedule</u> store

Using More Review Words

A Change each word by following the directions. Write each new word.

1. enjoy   minus **en**   plus **ous**   = _____
2. equally   minus **ly**   plus **un**   = _____
3. machinery   minus **ry**   plus **s**   = _____
4. bravery   minus **ry**   plus **ly**   = _____
5. export   minus **ex**   plus **able**   = _____
6. intend   minus **in**   plus **pre**   = _____
7. inject   minus **in**   plus **re**   = _____
8. subscription   minus **sub**   plus **pre**   = _____
9. nervous   minus **ous**   plus **un**   = _____
10. disagree   minus **dis**   plus **ment**   = _____
11. independent   minus **in, ent**   plus **able**   = _____
12. really   minus **ly**   plus **un**   = _____
13. inconsiderate   minus **in, ate**   plus **re**   = _____
14. chemical   plus **ly**   = _____
15. rely   plus **able**   = _____

B Three words in each row follow the same spelling pattern. One word does not. Write that word. Be ready to tell why it does not belong.

1. humorous   chorus   famous   joyous

2. chemical   annually   legally   normally

3. bakery   grocery   delivery   diary

4. dissatisfied   unnamed   inspect   unnumbered

5. destroy   enemy   really   satisfy

6. machinery   mechanic   anchor   school

7. alley   actually   delay   journey

8. convict   export   subject   victory

C Complete each analogy with a word from the box.

ridiculous	finally	stomach	nervous	ache
unnecessary	annually	rhinoceros	diary	echo

1. **friend** is to **enemy** as **calm** is to _____

2. **feel** is to **fur** as **hear** is to _____

3. **breathe** is to **lungs** as **digest** is to _____

4. **first** is to **originally** as **last** is to _____

5. **found** is to **lost** as **needed** is to _____

6. **rely** is to **depend** as **pain** is to _____

7. **tree** is to **oak** as **animal** is to _____

8. **money** is to **dime** as **book** is to _____

9. **funny** is to **humorous** as **silly** is to _____

10. **promptly** is to **punctually** as **yearly** is to _____

silent   belt   boarded   flown
taxied   soar   luggage   drank
propeller   soda   anxious   smooth
ramp   rack   relaxed   anymore
felt   fare   remainder   sitting

Prewriting. Prewriting is the thinking and planning you do before you begin to write. In this lesson, you will plan and write a **description**. You will imagine or remember a scene on an airplane or at an airport. Then you will use sense details to share the sight and feeling with others.

Use Prewriting Skills

A Answer these questions with spelling words. The words will help you think of ways to describe an airplane flight.

1. What two words describe opposite feelings about flying?

2. What word refers to the cost of the ticket?

3. What could you walk on to enter a plane?

4. What verb means "got on" a plane?

5. What verb tells how a plane moved on the ground?

6. What verb means "to fly upward"?

7. What must be buckled for the takeoff?

8. What helps to move some small planes forward?

9. What two-word phrase could refer to a storage area on a plane?

B To plan a description, you must decide exactly what scene you want to picture. Like a camera, you must focus on one location. This is called the viewpoint. For example, you might choose to describe the scene inside a plane. Or, you might focus on the scene inside an airport terminal.

Read these prewriting notes. Write the five details you could use to describe a scene inside a plane.

takeoff felt smooth
a row of gift shops
sitting in window seat
passengers never silent

cabs lined up outside
soft pillow on rack
scale for weighing luggage
drank cold soda during flight

C When you write a description, you must also decide what feeling or mood you want your description to have. The feeling might be one of excitement, happiness, fear, or calm, for example. Choose words that show this feeling. Make sure you keep the same feeling throughout the paragraph.

Rewrite each note. Choose the word in parentheses that helps to show a feeling of nervousness.

had (never, often) flown before
sitting (quietly, stiffly) for remainder of trip
hands (relaxed, clenched) during landing
felt (anxious, thrilled) about flying anymore

Now Think Make prewriting notes for your own description of an airplane flight. First decide what your viewpoint will be. Will you be inside the plane, outside the plane, or perhaps in the terminal? Imagine the scene. Experience it through your senses. Decide what feeling you want to express. Then as you jot down your thoughts, choose words that give that feeling.

Writing. To make a description clear to your readers, use specific details that appeal to the senses. The details should be in clear sentences. They should describe what you see, hear, smell, taste, and touch.

Use Writing Skills

Write the sense that each prewriting note appeals to. Then expand each phrase into a well-written sentence.

1. delicious ice-cold soda

2. seat felt rough and scratchy

3. fluffy, smooth white clouds

4. roar of the propeller

5. aroma of leather luggage

6. heels clip-clopping up the ramp

7. drank the hot chocolate

8. seat belt felt tight

9. voices became silent

10. hawk soared outside

Now Write   Look over your prewriting notes. Use them to write your description of an airplane flight or airport scene. Think of a good topic sentence. Tell what scene you are describing in your topic sentence. Then picture the scene as if you were looking at a photograph. Describe the scene through your senses. What general feeling does your description give? Is this feeling the same throughout?

Revising. When you revise, check to see if too many sentences begin the same way. Do most of them begin with **the** or **I**, for instance? If so, you can improve your writing by changing the pattern of some sentences.

> Example: The plane taxied down the runway.
> Down the runway taxied the plane.

Use Revising Skills

A Each sentence below begins with **the** or **I**. Revise each sentence by changing the order of the words.

1. The silver jet soared above the clouds.

2. The silent world grew smaller below the plane.

3. I wore my seat belt during the entire flight.

4. I slept soundly for the remainder of the trip.

5. The hum of the propeller droned through the window.

B Proofread the following descriptive paragraph. Find all the mistakes in capitalization, punctuation, and spelling. Then rewrite the paragraph correctly.

Remember
- Use a comma before **and** and **but** when they combine two sentences.
- Capitalize the names of organizations and institutions.
- Use an exclamation mark to show strong feeling.

Dozens of us stared at the long, black runway outside the airport window. At the far end, a dark spot appeared. It gradually turned into a small plane. We grew excited as the plane taxiied toward us. It stopped outside the window The propellors slowed down their spinning and the motor grew silunt. We watched anxiously as the stairs appeared. Out stepped the Carter high school champion basketball team.

C Revise the following first draft. These directions will help you. Then write the paragraph correctly on your own paper.

1. Find a sentence that doesn't belong to the scene being described.
2. Add sense details to describe the word **sky** in line 4.
3. Correct the capitalization errors in lines 5 and 10.
4. Find six misspelled words. Write them correctly.
5. Correct the punctuation errors in lines 2, 4, and 11.

1   Jenny was siting next to a window in the jumbo jet. She had never flown

2   before but the flight was smouth so far. She drank a soda as she relaxed and

3   looked out the window. The airport snack bar sold several flavors of soda.

4   Jenny enjoyed watching the fluffy clouds floating in the sky The clouds were

5   suddenly dark mist on the inside. she couldn't believe they were the same soft

6   pillows she had wanted to touch. Jenny could feel the plane descending as she

7   continued looking out the window. She noticed a bird sooring by. Far below a

8   marveleous patchwork design appeared. On it moved a row of moving objects.

9   It must be highway traffic. Now she was anxious for the remaneder of the trip to

10   be over. Soon she felt a bump and could see O'Hare airport in the distance.

11   She was almost sorry to see normal senery She would miss the sight of the tiny

12   world she had seen from the sky.

Now Revise   Now read the first draft of your own paragraph. Did you give details that can be observed through the senses? Did you use the best words for your purpose? Could this scene be pictured in a photograph or movie? Did you keep the same feeling throughout? Now proofread for mistakes in capitalization, punctuation, and spelling. Then copy your description over in your best handwriting.

Exchange descriptions with a friend. Compare your points of view and details. You will enjoy seeing how you have used the process of writing to paint a unique picture.

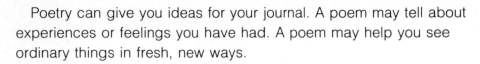

A Writer's Journal

Poetry can give you ideas for your journal. A poem may tell about experiences or feelings you have had. A poem may help you see ordinary things in fresh, new ways.

Let the poem in the box be a starting point for your next journal entry. Read the poem and think about what it means. Then discuss the questions with the class.

1. The speaker in the poem says "I'd like to be *you*." To whom is the speaker talking?

2. Why do you think the speaker in the poem wants to be someone else?

CHANGING

I know what *I* feel like;
I'd like to be *you*
And feel what *you* feel like
And do what *you* do.
I'd like to change places
For maybe a week
And look like your look-like
And speak as you speak
And think what you're thinking
And go where you go
And feel what you're feeling
And know what you know.
I wish we could do it;
What fun it would be
If I could try you out
And you could try me.

—MARY ANN HOBERMAN

Maybe the poem or the discussion has given you an idea for your journal. If so, start writing. If not, choose one of these ideas.

1. Think of someone whom you would like to be. He or she can be a famous person or someone you know well. Tell why you would like to be that person.

2. Imagine that you have changed places with a friend of yours. Try to describe what the friend is feeling or thinking at 7:30 AM, 12:30 PM, and 5:30 PM.

Spelling and Your Journal

There may be times when you are writing when you do not know how to spell a word you want to use. If this happens, follow these steps.

1. Write the word as you think it should be spelled.

2. After you have finished writing, check to see if the word is on the list you are keeping at the back of your journal. If not, look up the word in the dictionary.

3. Correct your spelling and add the word to your list.

4. Practice spelling the word several times.

VAC words

occur	*occurred*	*occurring*	*occurs*
control	*controlled*	*controlling*	*controls*
regret	*regretted*	*regretting*	*regrets*
permit	*permitted*	*permitting*	*permits*
patrol	*patrolled*	*patrolling*	*patrols*
transmit	*transmitted*	*transmitting*	*transmits*
expel	*expelled*	*expelling*	*expels*
omit	*omitted*	*omitting*	*omits*

A **VAC** word has a single vowel before a single consonant in an accented final syllable.

vowel   **c**onsonant

oc cúr

accented syllable

1. Are the eight words in column one **VAC** words?

2. What happens to the final consonant when **ed** or **ing** is added?

3. What happens to the final consonant when **s** is added?

Double the final consonant of a **VAC** word before adding a suffix that begins with a vowel. Do not double the final consonant before adding a suffix that begins with a consonant.

Practice the Words

Dictionary

A Each spelling word below is divided into two syllables. Say each word aloud and listen for the accented, or stressed, syllable. Copy the word and mark the accented syllable. Check your dictionary to make sure you are right.

B Write the **ed** and **ing** forms of each word.

1. trans·mit′

2. oc·cur

3. con·trol

4. o·mit

5. ex·pel

6. pa·trol

7. per·mit

8. re·gret

C Complete each sentence with the correct list word. Add correct tense endings following the **VAC** pattern.

1. The ship's radio _____ an urgent S.O.S.

2. He was _____ from the club for not paying his dues.

3. That strong dam _____ the flow of the river.

85

4. I accidentally _____ one answer on the science test.

5. The Coast Guard boat was _____ the bay.

6. Swimmers are not _____ to go beyond the ropes.

7. We _____ having the picnic on a rainy day.

8. Leap year _____ once every four years.

Build Word Power

Dictionary

Three spelling words contain the syllable **mit**, which comes from the Latin word meaning **send**. Many English words are made from this Latin root. Sometimes it is spelled **mis**, as in the word **mission**.

1. Write the definition of the word **mission**.

2. Change three spelling words into nouns that include the word **mission**. Find each noun in your dictionary and write the definition. Tell how each word is related to the meaning **send**.

1. permit
2. transmit
3. omit

occurred	controls	permitting	transmitted	expels
occurring	regretted	permits	transmitting	omitted
occurs	regretting	patrolled	transmits	omitting
controlled	regrets	patrolling	expelled	omits
controlling	permitted	patrols	expelling	

New Words

equip
propel
emit
submit
acquit

Reach Out for New Words

Writing

A Answer each question with a sentence that includes the **ed** form of a new **VAC** word.

1. What did the chimney do?

2. What did the jury do?

3. How was the firefighter prepared to fight the blaze?

4. What caused the rocket to blast into space?

5. Did every contestant turn in an entry form?

B Write the **ing** and **s** forms of each new word.

Look in your spelling dictionary to find the two new **VAC** words with a noun form that includes the word **mission**. Write these nouns.

Words ending with ary

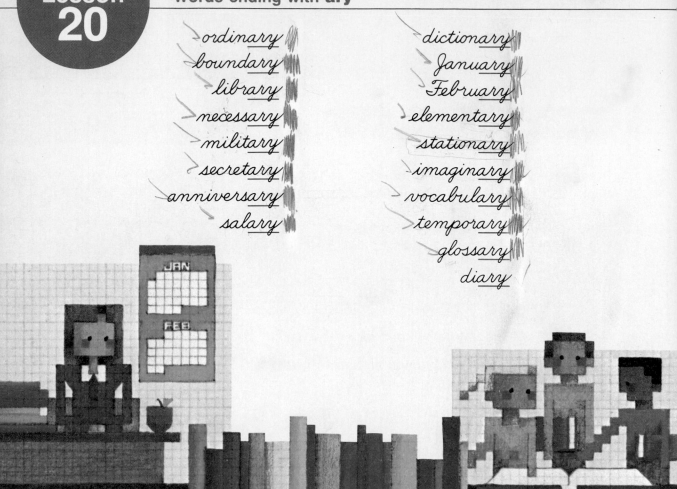

ordinary
boundary
library
necessary
military
secretary
anniversary
salary

dictionary
January
February
elementary
stationary
imaginary
vocabulary
temporary
glossary
diary

1. What are the last three letters of each word?
2. Can the letters **ry** be clearly heard?
3. Can the vowel before the **ry** be clearly heard and identified?
   What is this indistinct vowel?

The **ary** ending begins with a vowel that is not strongly accented or stressed.
   An unaccented vowel is hard to hear when it is followed by the letter **r**.
The ending **ary** can sound almost like **ery** in **very**. Remember that the ending
   ary is more common than **ery**.
   Mnemonic device: Remember the ordin**ary** **ary**.

Practice the Words

A Complete the sentences with the correct spelling words.

1. The book was about dragons and other _____ creatures.
2. Is that an _____ school or a junior high school?
3. No one noticed anything out of the _____.
4. New Year's Day is the first day of _____.
5. The new job offered a better _____.
6. My sister's job as _____ might be permanent or just _____.
7. Water is _____ for life to exist.
8. The north _____ of our property is clearly marked with stakes.
9. We borrowed books from the school _____.
10. Miguel wore his _____ uniform proudly.
11. Our parents celebrated their fifteenth _____.
12. This _____ of special words is in alphabetical order like a regular _____.
13. I have learned many new words from my _____ book.
14. Groundhog Day is celebrated in _____.
15. A cement base keeps the diving platform _____.

B Find the spelling words that fit in this puzzle.

						ary
						ary
			i			ary
				s		ary
		o				ary
					t	ary
			e			ary
		c				ary
	i					ary
		a				ary
						ary

Proofreading

C Find the eight misspelled words in the story. Write them correctly.

Anniversary Shop
Laundry Land
Vocabulary Print Shop

Sergeant Murphy was puzzled. This was no ordinairy case. The robberies had started in Januery with the Anniversry Shop and the Imaginery Images picture store. During Februery and March, there were sixteen more robberies. These included Laundry Land and Sam's Store.

Murphy checked the facts in her diery. Suddenly, she noticed that the robberies were in alphabetical order! Therefore, the next large firm to be robbed would be the Vocabulery Print Shop. Finally, Sergeant Murphy knew how to prevent the next robbery! Her puzzlement was only temperary.

Build Word Power

The letter **a** in **ary** is an indistinct vowel. It is hard to hear because it is in a syllable that is not <u>strongly</u> stressed or accented. When a vowel is in a strongly accented syllable, it is easier to hear. Sometimes a word will have another form in which the accent shifts to the indistinct vowel.

li′ brar·y   li·brar′ i·an

Dictionary

Write each base word on your paper. Find each base word in your spelling dictionary. Mark the accented syllable. Write the word formed by adding the suffix. Mark the accent on the newly formed word.

1. ordinary   + ly = _____   **4.** secretary + al = _____

2. necessary + ly = _____   **5.** temporary + ly = _____

3. military   + ly = _____

What happened to the unaccented letter **a**?

ordinary	military	dictionary	stationary	glossary
boundary	secretary	January	imaginary	diary
library	anniversary	February	vocabulary	
necessary	salary	elementary	temporary	

New Words

missionary
revolutionary
complimentary
extraordinary
contrary
sanitary

Reach Out for New Words

Dictionary

A Complete each sentence with one of the new **ary** words. Then find the word in your spelling dictionary. Write the part or parts of speech listed for each word. Then write the two guide words at the top of the dictionary page.

1. A solar eclipse is an _____ sight.

2. The judge's remarks to the winner were very _____ .

3. Scientists are searching for _____ new fuels for cars.

4. Restaurants must be kept _____ at all times.

5. The _____ described her work in foreign countries.

6. The defendant's story was _____ to the facts.

Writing

B A good newspaper story begins with a sentence that tells <u>who</u>, <u>what</u>, <u>where</u>, <u>when</u>, and <u>why</u>. This sentence is called the **lead**. Write two newspaper leads using two of your new **ary** words.

Yesterday afternoon, **revolutionary** forces in the Republic of Vanilla
    (when)   (who)   (where)

seized the government to protest the lack of chocolate.
    (what)   (why)

91

deceive

conceited

deceitful

receipt

ceiling

freight

weight

vein

reign

beige

their

neither

either

height

foreign

seized

protein

heir

1. What is the vowel combination that appears in each word?
2. In how many words does the **ei** combination follow the letter **c**?
3. In how many words does the **ei** sound like a long **a** as in **neighbor**?

The vowel combination **ei** appears in many words. It is used after the letter **c**. It is often used when the long **a** sound is heard.

Invent mnemonic devices to help you remember some of the common words on this list:

eight	**weight**	**either**	**reign**
h**eight**	fr**eight**	n**either**	fo**reign**

Practice the Words

A Find the word that fits in each shape. Then write the word.

1.
7.
13.

2.
8.
14.

3.
9.
15.

4.
10.
16.

5.
11.
17.

6.
12.
18.

B Complete the sentences with spelling words.

1. The _____ train had fifty boxcars.

2. Will you study a _____ language in high school?

3. A _____ carries blood to the heart.

4. Are your _____ and _____ average for your age?

5. The criminal was a _____ person.

6. People who brag are usually _____.

7. We used _____ paint on the walls and the _____.

8. Our bodies need _____ to be strong.

9. The tycoon's only _____ will inherit two million dollars.

C Make a word chain with seven spelling words. Each word begins with the last letter of the word before it. One letter has been filled in as a clue.

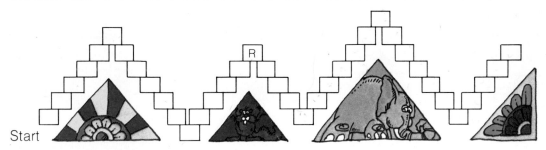

Start

Build Word Power

Homonyms are words that sound the same.

their-there   ceiling-sealing   heir-air

Homonyms do not have the same meaning.

Use your spelling dictionary to find three spelling words and their homonyms. The first letters have been given to help you.

Imagine how silly it would be

    if a queen could _n_

       and a cloud could _____,

    if a barn had a _r_

       and an arm had a _____,

    if scales told your _w_

       and a line had a _____.

Invent mnemonic devices for homonyms that confuse you.

deceive	ceiling	reign	either	protein
conceited	freight	beige	height	heir
deceitful	weight	their	foreign	
receipt	vein	neither	seized	

New Words
forfeit   leisure
weird   sleigh
heiress   counterfeit
veil

Reach Out for New Words

A Write the new **ei** words that fit the clues.

1. cloth worn on the head or face

2. strange or mysterious

3. time free from work

4. woman who inherits wealth

5. a snow vehicle or sled

6. lose by penalty

7. fake copy or imitation

Dictionary

B Read the dictionary entry for each new word. Follow the directions.

1. Add the **ly** suffix to make two of the words into adverbs.

2. Add the **es** plural to one of the nouns.

3. Write the **ed** and **ing** forms of four words that can be used as verbs.

4. Add the **un** prefix to one of the **ing** forms in question 3.

con + vince = *convince*

con + versation = *conversation*

con + dition = *condition*

con + test = *contest*

con + stitution = *constitution*

con + nect = *connect*

com + mon = *common*

com + mand = *command*

com + mit = *commit*

com + mercial = *commercial*

com + munity = *community*

com + ment = *comment*

com + plete = *complete*

com + pany = *company*

com + position = *composition*

com + bat = *combat*

com + puter = *computer*

com + pare = *compare*

The prefix **com** means "with" or "together." This prefix can be spelled in different ways. The spelling depends on the root to which the prefix is joined.

1. When the prefix **com** is joined to the first six roots, how is it spelled?
2. The next six roots begin with the letter **m**. How is **com** spelled when it is joined to these roots?
3. The last six roots begin with **p** or **b**. How is **com** spelled when it is joined to these roots?

The prefix **com** is spelled **con** before most letters of the alphabet.
   It is spelled **com** before roots that begin with the letters **m**, **p**, or **b**.
   It changes to make more compatible combinations that are easier to pronounce:
      Say both words out loud. **comdition → condition**
   Changing the last letter of the prefix often results in double consonants:
      co**nn**ect. Remember both letters when you write the word.
   Mnemonic device: Remember co**mm**on co**mp**atible co**mb**inations!

Practice the Words

A Complete the sentences with spelling words.

1. The best student _____ will be entered in the statewide essay _____.
2. The lawyer tried to _____ the jury that her client did not _____ the crime.
3. When did our country's founders _____ the final draft of the American _____?
4. The Army officer led the troops under his _____ into _____.
5. What is your favorite television _____?
6. As more _____ arrived at the party, the _____ became louder and livelier.
7. Is your bicycle in good _____ for the trip?
8. The bridge is needed to _____ the two parts of the _____.
9. Double consonants are the cause of many _____ spelling problems.
10. The announcer will _____ on the football game.
11. Our class is learning to operate a _____.
12. How did last year's fair _____ to this year's?

B Find the misspelled word in each group. Write the word correctly.

1. convince
   conect
   comment
   common

2. company
   condition
   conbat
   complete

3. commit
   connect
   convince
   comand

4. computer
   company
   conttest
   community

5. commercial
   command
   conversation
   conposition

6. constitution
   comercial
   compare
   condition

C Follow these directions using your spelling words.

1. Write the plural form of the two final **y** words.

2. Write the **ed** and **ing** forms of the three final silent **e** words.

3. Add the suffixes **ed** and **ing** to the **VAC** word **commit**.

4. Write the antonyms for three words by adding negative prefixes.

   dis   un   in

5. Change the meaning of one word by changing the prefix from **com** to **dis**.

6. Change three nouns to adjectives by adding **al**.

Build Word Power

Writing

A cinquain is a five-line poem.

Line 1   one noun

Line 2   two words related to the noun

Line 3   three action words related to the noun

Line 4   four words giving an idea or feeling about the noun

Line 5   a noun that relates to the first word

Composition

Thinking, writing

Editing, proofreading, revising

Shaping ideas into words

Creation

Write two cinquains. Use a spelling word for the first word in each poem.

convince ✓   constitution   commit   complete ✓   computer

conversation   connect   commercial   company   compare ✓

condition   common   community ✓   composition

contest   command   comment   combat

New Words
Discover new words below!

Reach Out for New Words

A Build a word pyramid by following the code. Use your spelling dictionary to find the four pyramid words that match the definitions.

> The root **ver** means "turn."

1. turn upside down

2. turn back

3. "turn under," or overthrow

4. able to be turned or changed

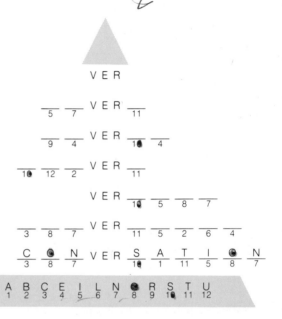

B Build another word pyramid. Use your spelling dictionary to find the four pyramid words that match the definitions.

> The root **pos** means "put" or "place."

1. to put into place

2. the act of putting away or getting rid of

3. a person or group "put against" another

4. the way parts are put together

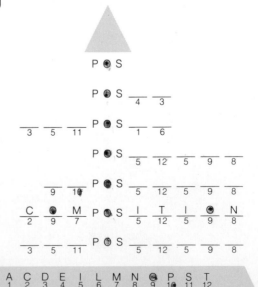

99

Forms of the prefix ad

13 ad + mit = *admit* ✓
7 ad + vice = *advice* ✓
9 ad + verb = *adverb* ✓
14 ad + jective = *adjective* ✓
1 ad + hesive = *adhesive* ✓
2 ad + vance = *advance* ✓
8 ad + opt = *adopt* ✓
6 ad + ult = *adult* ✓
ad + dition = *addition*

ar + range = *arrange* ✓
1 ar + rival = *arrival* ✓

12 ac + cent = *accent* ✓
3 ac + cident = *accident* ✓
4 ac + complished = *accomplished* ✓
11 as + sembly = *assembly* ✓
10 as + sist = *assist* ✓
as + signment = *assignment*
as + sortment = *assortment*

The prefix **ad** means "to," "toward," or "near." This prefix can be spelled in different ways. The spelling depends on the root to which the prefix is joined.

1. In the first nine words, does the spelling of the prefix **ad** change when it is added to the roots? How many of the roots begin with the letter **d**, causing a double consonant in the word?

2. What happens to the spelling of **ad** when it is joined to roots that begin with the letter **r**? What happens to **ad** when the root begins with a **c**? What happens to **ad** when the root begins with an **s**?

The prefix **ad** often changes to match the first letter of a root. This prefix causes more double consonants than any other prefix.

     ad becomes **ar** before the letter **r**
     ad becomes **as** before the letter **s**
     ad becomes **ac** before the letter **c**
Don't drop one of the two consonants!

A Find the spelling words that fit in the puzzle.

Across
1. the reaching of a place
2. to move forward
4. completed
7. information, opinion
8. take into a family
9. can modify a verb
11. a group meeting
12. an extra force or stress
13. to allow to enter
14. can modify a noun

Down
1. a sticky substance
3. an unintentional happening
5. to place in a certain order
6. grown-up
10. to help

Writing

B Unscramble the sentences and write them correctly. Capitalize the first word. Underline the spelling words.

1. choose to child some adults a adopt.
2. sentences boring adjectives admit I would be without adverbs and.
3. assembly assignment her during lost Lori addition the.
4. accident the covered tape was after assortment an of Fred adhesive with.

C Unscramble the syllables to make spelling words. There is an extra syllable or syllables in each group.

1. cent vince ac
2. verb ment sign as
3. al mit sem ad
4. sort ad ment vice
5. di ci tion ad
6. ac plished sist com
7. ar sort al riv
8. ad ac verb tive
9. ac range ci ar
10. ment as sem sort
11. tive ad ac jec
12. as ac ad sist
13. vance ad tion

Build Word Power

Dictionary

Alphabetize the ten words with double consonants. Divide each word into syllables and mark the accent. Then write another form of each word by adding or changing a suffix. Use your spelling dictionary to help you. Remember, word forms may be separate entries or within other entries.

admit   adhesive   addition①   accident⑤   assignment⑨   **New Words**
advice   advance   arrange②   accomplished②   assortment⑩   Discover
adverb   adopt   arrival③   assembly⑦   new words
adjective   adult   accent④   assist⑧   below!

Reach Out for New Words

A Build a word pyramid by following the code. Use your spelling dictionary to find the four pyramid words that match the definitions.

> The root **jec** means "throw."

1. to throw back

2. something "thrown" into the body

3. something "thrown" in between

4. throw out of or away from

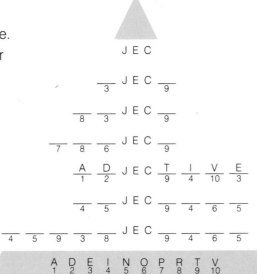

B Build another word pyramid. Use your spelling dictionary to find the four pyramid words that match the definitions.

> The root **mit** means "send" or "let go."

1. let something go; leave out

2. something sent back to

3. sent through or allowed

4. a group of people "sent" together

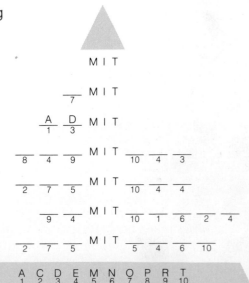

singular ✓
regular ✓
rectangular ✓
particular ✓
muscular ✓
popular ✓
circular ✓
spectacular ✓

similar ✓
burglar ✓
solar ✓
polar ✓
cellar ✓
collar ✓
dollar ✓

grammar ✓
calendar ✓
lunar ✓

1. What are the last four letters of the first eight words?

2. What letter comes before the **ar** ending in fifteen of the eighteen spelling words?

The ending **ar** is a noun or adjective ending that often comes after the letter **l**.

Dictionary

A Use your spelling dictionary to divide each word into syllables. Mark the accented syllable.

How many of the words are accented on the last syllable?

Because the **ar** is not in an accented syllable, the vowel before the final **r** is an indistinct vowel and hard to identify. Sometimes it can be heard more clearly in another form of the word:

gram′ mar   gram·ma′ti·cal

The mystery vowel is no longer a mystery when it is in an accented syllable.

B Write the words formed by adding the **ity** ending. Mark the accented syllable. Say each word aloud to hear the change in pronunciation.

1. similar   + ity = _____

2. regular   + ity = _____

3. singular   + ity = _____

4. popular   + ity = _____

5. muscular + ity = _____

6. circular   + ity = _____

C Use the shapes and the clues to find spelling words. Each clue contains an easy **ar** word to remind you of the spelling word.

1. shape of a card

2. dark place

3. from our star, the sun

4. might set off an alarm

5. worn around the neck

6. special part or thing

7. spent in a market

8. marks days of a year

9. includes parts of speech

10. marvelous

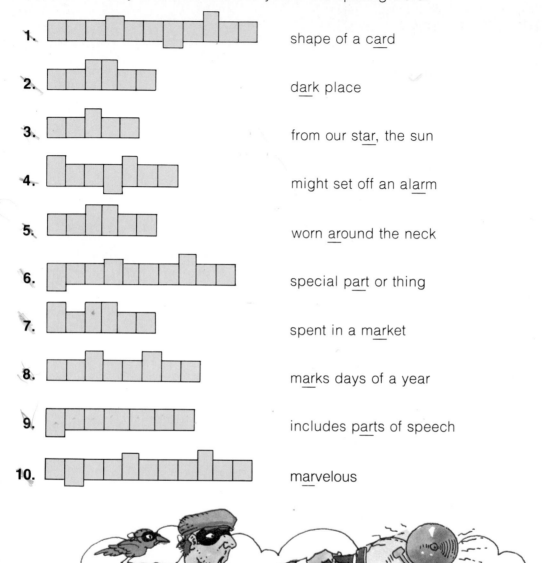

Build Word Power

Writing

Change five spelling words to adverbs by adding the **ly** suffix. Look at the definitions in your spelling dictionary. Then make a phrase by writing either a verb, adjective, or adverb after each **ly** word.

singular	muscular	similar	cellar	calendar
regular	popular	burglar	collar	lunar
rectangular	circular	solar	dollar	
particular	spectacular	polar	grammar	

New Words
Discover
new words
below!

Reach Out for New Words

A Find eight new words that end with **ar** in these telephone directory ads. Write the words. Some of the words may be in their plural form.

Fantastic Village

Visit the world of tomorrow today. Come to our model village. Everything runs on atomic or ~~nuclear~~ energy. Reservations at 555-6666.

Glass Houses

We cut glass to any shape no matter how ~~peculiar~~. Square, oblong, or round. You design it—we cut it. 555-9473.

Marble Masterpieces

Imported marble for all purposes. We make mantles, altars, and perpendicular pillars to your design. 555-6678.

To Your Health

We have a wide variety of health foods: unbleached flour, imported vinegar, much more. Call today. 555-0375.

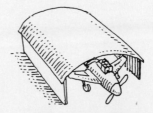

Hasty Hangar Co.

Pre-fab airplane hangars while you wait. Take off, circle the field for an hour, and return to your own familiar monogrammed hangar! 555-3456.

Writing

Make your own telephone ads with some of your new **ar** words. Check your local directory for ideas.

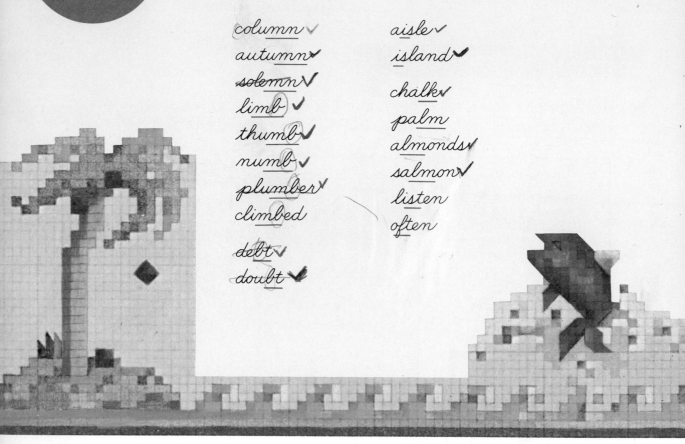

column ✓   aisle ✓
autumn ✓   island ✓
solemn ✓   chalk ✓
limb ✓   palm
thumb ✓   almonds ✓
numb ✓   salmon ✓
plumber ✓   listen
climbed   often

debt ✓
doubt ✓

Look at the underlined letters in each word. Only one of the two letters is pronounced. The other letter is a "silent partner."

1. The letter **m** has two silent partners in the first eight words. What are those letters?
2. What is the silent letter in **debt** and **doubt?**
3. What silent letter is in both **aisle** and **island**?
4. What is the silent letter in the next four words?
5. What is the silent letter in **listen** and **often**?

A few consonants are silent in certain combinations.
      mn   mb   bt   lk   lm   isl

Practice the Words

A Write the correct spelling words.

   1. Write the seven spelling words that have a silent **b**.
   2. Write the four words that have a silent **l**.
   3. Write the three words that have a silent **n**.
   4. Write the two words that have a silent **s**.
   5. Write the two words that have a silent **t**.

B Complete the sentences with spelling words.

   1. Do you like ＿＿ in a chocolate bar?
   2. The ＿＿ squeaked on the blackboard.
   3. We took a power boat from the mainland to the ＿＿.
   4. When do the ＿＿ swim upriver?
   5. ＿＿ is my favorite season of the year.
   6. I knew something was wrong when I saw the ＿＿ look on Sue's face.
   7. The usher led us down the dark ＿＿ of the theater.
   8. Sean's mother writes a ＿＿ for the newspaper.
   9. The gardener had a "green ＿＿."
   10. The ＿＿ of the young tree broke in the storm.
   11. My bruised finger lost its feeling and became ＿＿.
   12. The ＿＿ fixed the clogged drain.
   13. Jack paid the ＿＿ as soon as he had the money.
   14. If you are in ＿＿ about the directions, ask for help.
   15. Carmen scraped the ＿＿ of her hand.

C Every other letter is missing in the spelling words. Add the missing letters and write each word.

1. p __ u __ b __ r
2. s __ l __ m __
3. d __ u __ t
4. p __ l __
5. n __ m __
6. d __ b __

7. a __ s __ e
8. a __ t __ m __
9. l __ s __ e __
10. s __ l __ o __
11. l __ m __
12. a __ m __ n __ s

13. i __ l __ n __
14. c __ l __ m __
15. t __ u __ b
16. c __ a __ k
17. o __ t __ n
18. c __ i __ b __ d

Build Word Power

Writing

Write acrostic poems with two or more of your spelling words.

No feeling
Under
My
Bruised thumb.

Let's all climb
Into the leaves of
My tree and sit in the
Branches all day.

column	thumb	debt	chalk	listen
autumn	numb	doubt	palm	often
solemn	plumber	aisle	almonds	
limb	climbed	island	salmon	

New Words

knock	crumb
thighs	knees
wrist	knife
whole	comb
raspberry	knuckles

Reach Out for New Words

A Find the old and new words in the poem that have silent consonants.

Your Silent Letter Life

You depend on your thighs and your knees to walk,
Your knuckles to knock, and your mouth to talk.
You hold a knife and fork with your palm and thumb
to eat spaghetti and salmon without losing a crumb,
or all the rhubarb and raspberry pie you can bake
and eat without getting a stomachache.
You twist your wrist to comb your hair,
and move your limbs to climb a stair.
Your whole life depends, no doubt it's true,
On silent letters—can you find 22?

B Group the silent letter words you have found in the poem. Write each word under the correct heading.

Silent k	**Silent l**	**Silent h**	**Silent p**
(4 words)	(4 words)	(4 words)	(1 word)

Silent b	**Silent w**	**Silent gh**	
(6 words)	(2 words)	(1 word)	

Circle the words that name a part of your body.

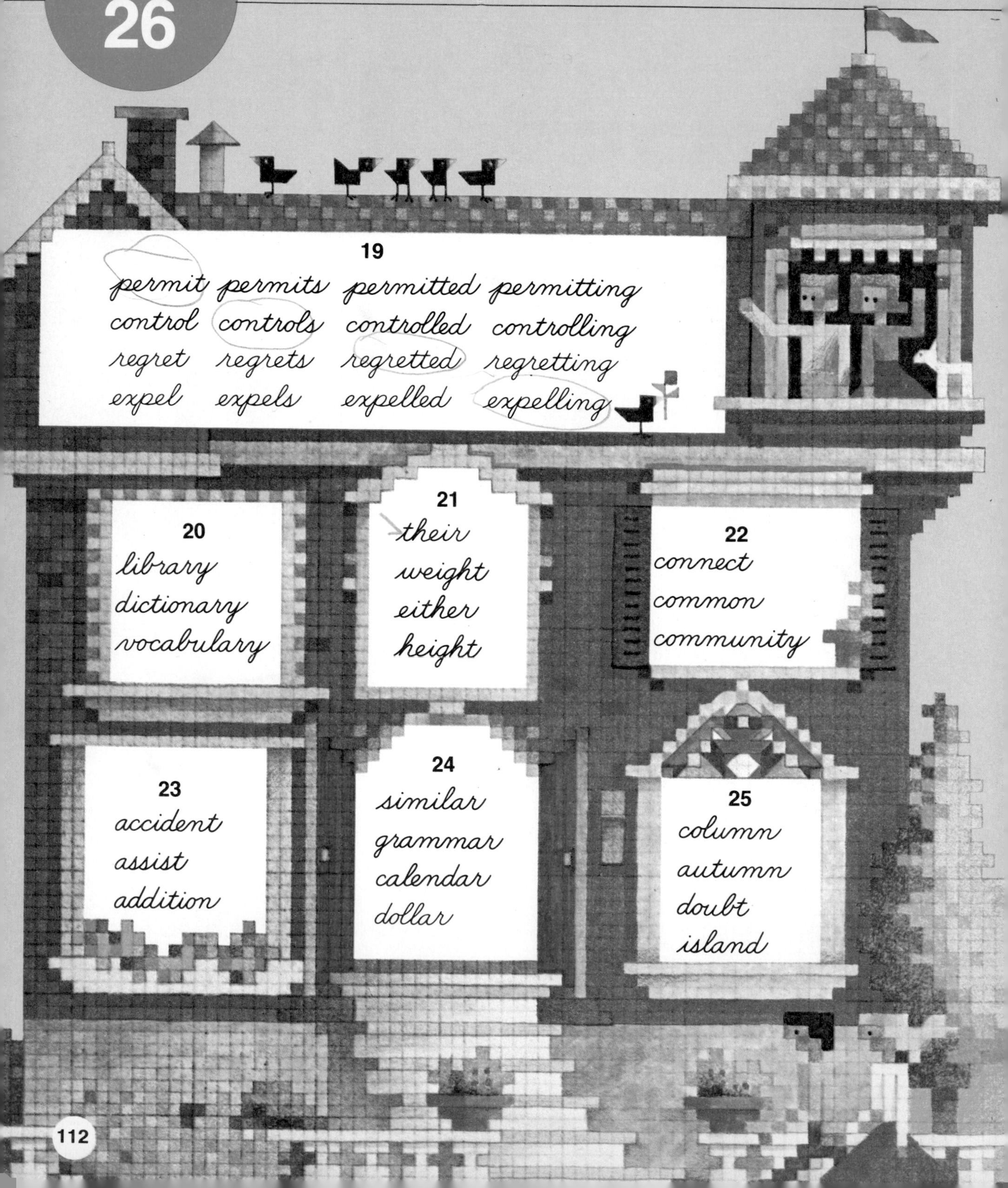

19

permit permits permitted permitting
control controls controlled controlling
regret regrets regretted regretting
expel expels expelled expelling

20
library
dictionary
vocabulary

21
their
weight
either
height

22
connect
common
community

23
accident
assist
addition

24
similar
grammar
calendar
dollar

25
column
autumn
doubt
island

Using Review Words

A Complete each analogy with the correct form of a spelling word.

1. **companies** is to **company** as **communities** is to _____

2. **here** is to **hear** as **there** is to _____

3. **commanded** is to **command** as **connected** is to _____

4. **regret** is to **regretted** as **permit** is to _____

5. **accidental** is to **accident** as **additional** is to _____

6. **patrol** is to **patrolled** as **expel** is to _____

7. **remit** is to **admit** as **resist** is to _____

8. **hopeful** is to **hope** as **doubtful** is to _____

9. **thumbs** is to **thumb** as **columns** is to _____

10. **occur** is to **occurred** as **regret** is to _____

11. **completely** is to **complete** as **commonly** is to _____

12. **permit** is to **permitting** as **control** is to _____

B Write spelling words to complete the paragraph.

Tricia's family was packing for _____ first trip to a tropical _____ owned by a foreign country. She had checked out books from the _____ to read about the customs. She had also bought a pocket _____ of the language. The dictionary didn't teach any _____ rules, but it did help her to learn some common _____ words. She had no _____ that she would make many mistakes, and hoped that people would _____ her.

Tricia packed carefully because of the airline's _____ limit. _____ her radio or her jacket would have to come out of the crowded suitcase. She could hardly _____ her excitement as she finally snapped the suitcase closed. The special day marked in red on her _____ had arrived at last!

C One word in each group is misspelled. Find the misspelled word and write it correctly.

 1. familiar
~~similiar~~
column
doubt

 2. ~~hieght~~
assist
common
island

 3. addition
permitted
~~doller~~
their

 4. dictionary
community
controlled
~~autunm~~

 5. calendar
either
autumn
~~conect~~

 6. vocabulary
~~acident~~
weight
traveled

Using More Review Words

Follow the directions to make other forms of spelling words.

1. adverb   minus **ad**   plus **ally**   = _____
2. similar   minus **ar**   plus **e**   = _____
3. compare   minus **e**   plus **ison**   = _____
4. addition   minus **ad**   plus **con**   = _____
5. imaginary   minus **ary**   plus **ation**   = _____
6. accident   minus **ac**   plus **in**   = _____
7. popular   minus **ar**   plus **ation**   = _____
8. constitution   minus **con**   plus **in**   = _____
9. commercial   minus **ial**   plus **e**   = _____
10. receipt   minus **pt**   plus **ve**   = _____
11. adhesive   minus **ad**   plus **co**   = _____
12. company   minus **y**   plus **ion**   = _____
13. regular   minus **ar**   plus **ation**   = _____
14. connect   plus **ion**   = _____
15. limb   plus **er**   = _____
16. debt   plus **or**   = _____
17. vocabulary   minus **bulary**   plus **l**   = _____
18. numb   plus **ness**   = _____

B Three words In each row follow the same spelling pattern. Write the word that does not follow the pattern. Be ready to tell why it does not belong.

1. foreign	circular	seized	receipt
2. command	collar	commit	commercial
3. limb	thumb	adverb	numb
4. regret	control	expel	listen
5. autumn	assist	accent	assembly
6. regular	grammar	salary	calendar
7. plumber	doubt	climbed	combat
8. chalk	solar	aisle	salmon
9. community	boundary	necessary	military
10. advice	accomplish	almonds	adhesive

C Complete each analogy with a spelling word from the box.

island	calendar	rectangular	singular
weight	similar	adverb	either
common	conversation	ceiling	chalk

1. **antonym** is to **different** as **synonym** is to _____

2. **nor** is to **neither** as **or** is to _____

3. **noun** is to **adjective** as **verb** is to _____

4. **ocean** is to **pond** as **continent** is to _____

5. **color** is to **blue** as **shape** is to _____

6. **writing** is to **composition** as **speaking** is to _____

7. **hours** is to **clock** as **week** is to _____

8. **down** is to **floor** as **up** is to _____

9. **inches** is to **height** as **pounds** is to _____

10. **paper** is to **pen** as **blackboard** is to _____

11. **muscle** is to **muscular** as **single** is to _____

12. **extraordinary** is to **rare** as **ordinary** is to _____

SPELLING AND THE PROCESS OF WRITING

spacecraft   silver   fuel ✓   surface
steering ✓   worse   risk ✓   degrees ✓
shuttle ✓   orbit ✓   shot   glimpse ✓
problem   crust ✓   crew   gauge
further   solid   lack ✓   planet ✓

Prewriting. Prewriting is the thinking and planning you do before you begin to write. In this lesson, you are going to plan and write a **story**. Your story will be about imaginary people or creatures who live in a world different from the real world. This kind of story is called **fantasy**.

Use Prewriting Skills

A Answer the questions with spelling words. The words will help you think of ideas about an imaginary adventure such as a journey in space.

1. What two more specific words could you use in place of **driving** a **vehicle**?
   _____ a _____

2. What word names a spacecraft that goes back and forth over short distances?

3. Where might a spacecraft travel to?

4. What word means "to go around a planet"?

5. What two words could suggest a "shortage of energy" on the spacecraft?
   _____ of _____

6. What are two words that refer to the outer layer of a planet?

7. What instrument for measuring might be on a spacecraft?
   What unit of measurement might it use?

8. What word could refer to a "quick look" at a shooting star?

9. What is another word for the chance you take in a new adventure?

B To write a story, first decide whom you want to write about. This will be your **main character**. You might choose to write about a boy or girl like yourself, an animal, a plant, or an imaginary creature. Here is a list of possible main characters. Find and write those that could exist only in fantasy, not in the real world.

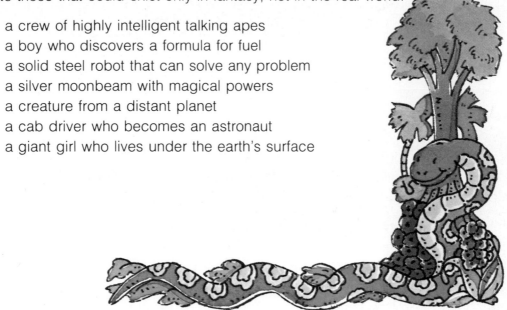

a crew of highly intelligent talking apes
a boy who discovers a formula for fuel
a solid steel robot that can solve any problem
a silver moonbeam with magical powers
a creature from a distant planet
a cab driver who becomes an astronaut
a giant girl who lives under the earth's surface

C Now you must decide what your **plot** will be. The plot is what happens to your characters.

Here is a list of plot ideas. Choose one to use with each one of the imaginary characters you identified in the exercise above. Write the plot idea below the description of the character.

rescues a spacecraft that has fallen out of orbit
is shot further into space than anyone has ever gone
risks capture to save a boy and his dog from drowning
escapes one evil tyrant but has worse luck with another
raises Earth's temperature ten degrees

Now Think Make prewriting notes for your own story. Begin by making a list of possible characters. Plan your plot by adding ideas about what might happen to each character. Then choose one set of ideas for your story.

Writing. A story has three parts: the introductory paragraph, the body, and the ending. The introductory paragraph usually tells **who** the story is about. It tells **where** the story takes place, and gives some idea of **what** will happen in the story. The body tells the important events of the story. The ending ties up the loose ends.

Use Writing Skills

Read this introductory paragraph to a story. It should tell **who**, **where**, and **what** about the story. Decide which part is missing. Rewrite the paragraph. Make up and add details to supply the missing information.

> The silver ship shot up from the bottom of the ocean. It broke the surface of the water with a gigantic spray. Then, like a shooting star going backwards, it sped further and further away from the planet Mars. The flight to Earth was going smoothly when suddenly a problem developed. The spacecraft began falling out of orbit. A quick glimpse at the gauge revealed that the ship was losing fuel.

Now Write

Use your prewriting notes to write a fantasy. In the first paragraph, tell who the characters are and where the story takes place. Give some idea of what the story is about. In the body, tell what happens to the characters. Write a good final paragraph that brings the story to a close.

Revising. The body of a story tells what happens. These events should be told in a **time sequence**. They tell what happened in the order that it happened. When you revise your story, make sure you have told the events in the correct order.

Use Revising Skills

A The following paragraph is from the body of a story. Some of the events are out of order. Revise the paragraph by writing it in the correct order.

As it neared Earth, the spacecraft slowed down. The vehicle shot through space at high speeds. The two sea creatures inside wondered if there was water below. Misty carefully checked the Planet Composition Detector. The gauge showed the location of a large body of water. Foam prepared to descend. He guided the ship below the surface of the water. He took control of the steering device. The sea creatures opened the hatch and swam out.

B Proofread this part of the story for mistakes in grammar, capitalization, punctuation, and spelling. Then rewrite the paragraph correctly.

Remember
- Make sure verbs agree with their subjects in number.
- Capitalize proper adjectives, such as in Martian atmosphere.
- Use an apostrophe to show possession, as in a boy's dream.

Misty and Foam climbed on the surfase of a rock to rest. Suddenly they caught a glimse of Earth people. But where was the peoples flippers? Were these the legendary humans that sea creatures had heard stories about.

C Revise the following introduction and body paragraph of a story. The directions below will help you. Then make a corrected copy on your own paper.

1. In the introductory paragraph, one part is missing. Make it up and write it.
2. Find the sentence in the second paragraph that does not follow the time sequence. Write it where it belongs.
3. Find six misspelled words. Write them correctly.
4. Correct the error in verb agreement in line 2 and the capitalization error in line 9.
5. Correct two punctuation errors in line 10.

1   The time machine stood ready for testing. For two years Jeff had watched

2   his mother solve every problum in its construction. They both knew they was

3   taking a risk in this test. They were going to atempt to travel from 1985 to 1942.

4   Mom set the guage. Soon they could feel themselves spinning.

5   After a long while, a picture appeared on their viewscreen. Suddenly two

6   huge dinosaurs moved through the trees. They had traveled too far back in

7   time! Jeff and his mother saw a solid wall of trees on the screen. Jeff quickly

8   addjusted the controls. The machine lurched forward. This time they caught a

9   glimpse of a sliver spacecraft. On the side was the name saturn Shuttle. Just

10   then their stearing wheel froze Would they be stuck in the future.

Now Revise

Read the first draft of your own story. Does your introductory paragraph tell who, where, and what about the story? Are all the sentences in the body in the correct time sequence? Did you tie up loose ends in the ending paragraph? Remember to proofread for mistakes in grammar, capitalization, punctuation, and spelling. Then make the final copy in your best handwriting.

When you finish, share your story with someone. Show them how the process of writing has helped you create a fantasy.

A Writer's Journal

UNIT FOUR

Read the poem. Think about what it is saying. Then read the questions about the poem. Discuss possible answers with your class.

SEPTEMBER

The breezes taste
   Of apple peel.
The air is full
   Of smells to feel—

Ripe fruit, old footballs,
   Burning brush,
New books, erasers,
   Chalk, and such.

The bee, his hive
   Well-honeyed, hums,
And Mother cuts
   Chrysanthemums.

Like plates washed clean
   With suds, the days
Are polished with
   A morning haze.

          —JOHN UPDIKE

1. What does the poet mean when he says, "The air is full of smells to feel"? How can a person feel smells?

2. Many people think of school when they think of September. Which lines of the poem tell about things that have to do with school?

Now use the poem as a starting point for your next journal entry. Here are some ideas you might want to use.

1. In the poem, the poet names many things that remind him of the month of September. Make your own list of all the things that September means to you. If you wish, you may write your list in the form of a poem.

2. Name your favorite month of the year. Tell what it is about the month that makes it special for you.

Spelling and Your Journal

When you are writing, there may be times when you do not know how to spell a word you want to use. When this occurs, follow these steps.

1. Write the word as you think it should be spelled.

2. After you have finished writing, check to see if the word is on the list you are keeping at the back of your journal. If not, look up the word in the dictionary.

3. Correct your spelling and add the word to your list.

4. Practice spelling the word several times.

Greek combining forms

tele + graph = *telegraph*

geo + graphy = *geography*

photo + graph = *photograph*

bio + graphy = *biography*

auto + graph = *autograph*

phono + graph = *phonograph*

auto + bio + graphy = *autobiography*

auto + mobile = *automobile*

auto + matic = *automatic*

tele + phone = *telephone*

mega + phone = *megaphone*

micro + phone = *microphone*

micro + scope = *microscope*

tele + scope = *telescope*

tele + vision = *television*

tele + pathy = *telepathy*

sym + pathy = *sympathy*

sym + phony = *symphony*

Look at the Greek combining forms before they are joined to make words.

1. How many times is some form of **graph** used?
What eight word parts are used more than once?

2. Forms of the word part **phone** are used five times.
Are they used as the first or the second part of words?

> Greek word parts can be combined in different ways to make
> English words. They are joined in almost the same way as
> English words are joined to make compound words.
> touchdown   downstairs   telephone   phonograph
> Knowing the meaning of the separate parts will help you to
> understand the many words made by combining the parts.

Practice the Words

A Complete the sentences with spelling words.

1. Alexander Graham Bell invented the _____.
2. Students learn about the earth's surface in _____ books.
3. Marconi invented the "wireless" message, or the _____.
4. The performer needed a _____ to be heard in the large theater.
5. Henry Ford was a leader in the early _____ industry.
6. Cells that are invisible to the eye can be seen with a _____.
7. _____ provides inexpensive, convenient home entertainment.
8. Today's record industry began with Edison's invention of the _____.
9. I plan to put all my snapshots in a _____ album.
10. A _____ contains important facts about a person's life.
11. Only skilled musicians perform in the _____ orchestra.
12. We were able to see Mars through the _____.
13. Famous people sometimes write an _____.
14. The fans were quiet out of _____ for the injured player.
15. We asked the famous actress for her _____.
16. Each cheerleader yelled through a _____.
17. Some people try to communicate ideas by mental _____.
18. The door has an _____ control which opens and closes it.

B Look at the meanings of these Greek word parts. Then write the spelling words made by combining the meanings.

phone = sound	tele = far	scope = view	mega = big
graph = writing	photo = light	mobile = moving	matic = work, act
micro = small	auto = self	pathy = feel	vision = see
bio = life	sym = together, with	geo = earth	

1. small + view = _____
2. far + view = _____
3. far + sound = _____
4. self + writing = _____
5. together + feel = _____
6. self + moving = _____
7. earth + writing = _____
8. sound + writing = _____

9. far + writing = _____

10. life + writing = _____

11. small + sound = _____

12. big + sound = _____

13. far + feel = _____

14. light + writing = _____

15. together + sound = _____

16. self + life + writing = _____

17. far + see = _____

18. self + work = _____

Dictionary

A dictionary may show the history of some words in a special note called an **etymology**.

C Read the etymology of the word **telephone** in your spelling dictionary. It is shown below the entry.

1. The word **telephone** comes from two Greek word parts. Write each word part and its meaning.

2. Who invented the telephone?

3. In what year was the telephone invented?

Someday we will have a telephone that lets us see the person who is talking to us. Use Greek word parts to make up a name for it.

Build Word Power

Some Greek forms have been made into English words simply by adding a suffix. Find the meaning of these English words in your spelling dictionary.

phonics   graphic

The **ic** suffix is added to form adjectives meaning "like" or "connected with." Add the **ic** suffix to these spelling words. Use the rules for adding suffixes to words with a final **y** or final silent **e**. Then write a noun after each new adjective to make a phrase.

1. photograph   2. microscope   3. geography   4. symphony

telegraph	autograph	automatic	microscope	sympathy
geography	phonograph	telephone	telescope	symphony
photograph	autobiography	megaphone	television	
biography	automobile	microphone	telepathy	

New Words
perimeter
optometry
thermometer
diameter
geometry
barometer

Reach Out for New Words

Meter is a Greek combining form that means **measure**.

The spelling may be changed to **metry** or **metric**, just as the endings of English words change. **Meter** combines with other word parts to make many common words.

Dictionary

A Find the meaning of each word part in your spelling dictionary. Write the meaning. Then write the word that can be made by combining the word part with **meter**.

1. thermo
2. dia
3. peri

4. baro
5. opto
6. geo

Writing

B Write four of your new words. Read the definition for each in your spelling dictionary. Write a sentence that shows the connection between the word and what it is used to measure.

125

Compound words and contractions

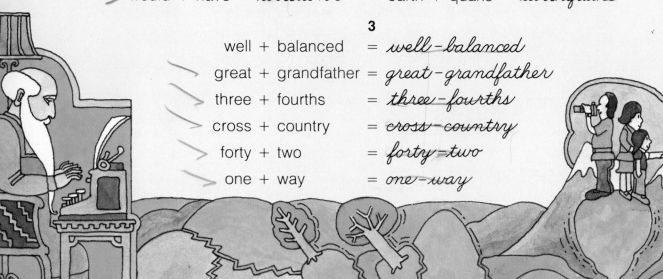

1

it + is	=	*it's*
who + is	=	*who's*
there + is	=	*there's*
can + not	=	*can't*
they + are	=	*they're*
would + have	=	*would've*

2

type + writer	=	*typewriter*
sight + seers	=	*sightseers*
room + mate	=	*roommate*
life + guard	=	*lifeguard*
night + time	=	*nighttime*
earth + quake	=	*earthquake*

3

well + balanced	=	*well-balanced*
great + grandfather	=	*great-grandfather*
three + fourths	=	*three-fourths*
cross + country	=	*cross-country*
forty + two	=	*forty-two*
one + way	=	*one-way*

1. In the first group of words, what was added when the words were joined? For what purpose is the apostrophe used in these words?

2. In the second group of words, was anything added or dropped when the words were joined?
Why do **roommate** and **nighttime** have double letters?

3. What was added when the words in the last group were joined?

Words can be joined together in several ways.
- When an apostrophe is used to show that one or more letters have been omitted, the word is called a **contraction**.
- When two or more words are simply connected with no changes, the word is called a **compound word**.
- Words joined by a hyphen are another kind of compound word.

Practice the Words

A Find the words that fit in the shapes. Count a space for apostrophes
and hyphens. Write each word.

1.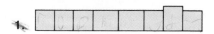

9.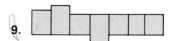

2.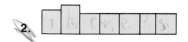

10.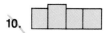

3.

11.

4.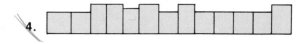

12.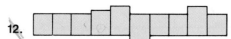

5.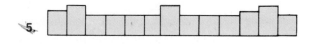

13.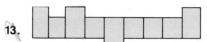

6.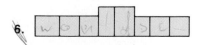

14.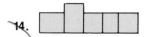

7.

15.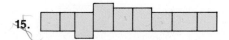

8.

16.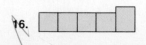

127

Writing

B Write possessive phrases. Punctuate each noun to make it show ownership. Add words after each noun to tell what is "owned."

1. sightseers

2. great-grandfather

3. roommate

4. typewriter

C Use one contraction, one compound word, and one hyphenated compound word to complete each sentence. Use each spelling word only once.

1. Who _____ believed that an _____ could topple a _____ story building?

2. _____ an antique _____ that once belonged to my _____ .

3. _____ _____ from California who have traveled _____ to see the Capitol.

4. _____ brave enough to walk _____ of a mile through these woods at _____ ?

5. My brother's _____ believes that _____ important to eat _____ meals.

6. The _____ _____ allow us to swim in both directions in the _____ lanes.

Build Word Power

Write the spelling word that is a homonym for each word. Then complete each sentence with the correct spelling of the homonyms.

1. whose   _____ book is this?

                    _____ going to the movie?

2. there   _____ not going.

                    _____ isn't any paint left.

3. theirs   _____ a squirrel in that tree.

                 The ball is _____ , not ours.

4. its   The puppy chased _____ tail.

                 _____ almost time for lunch.

it's	they're	roommate	well-balanced	forty-two
who's	would've	lifeguard	great-grandfather	one-way
there's	typewriter	nighttime	three-fourths	
can't	sightseers	earthquake	cross-country	

New Words
Discover
new words
below!

Reach Out for New Words

A All of the word parts have been joined in the same way to make silly
words. Rematch them to make **contractions**, **compound words**, and
hyphenated compounds. Check the spelling in your dictionary. Tell
what kind of word each one is after you have written it.

Change only the underlined parts. Use each part only once.

1. wholeshelf
2. selfis
3. twentyback
4. sheinlaw
5. tenboard

6. brotherfive
7. surfare
8. bookspeed
9. hatchsale
10. youaddressed

...ng

...o sentences with your new words. Use a contraction, a
...nd word, and a hyphenated word in each sentence.

129

Words spelled with **or**

navigator   honor
visitor   color
doctor   favor
actor   flavor
editor   rumor
director   error
operator   mirror
inventor   terror
   horror
   equator

1. What are the last two letters of all the spelling words?
Which of these two letters is an indistinct letter?
Is the last syllable in each word accented or unaccented?

2. The first eight words are alike in two ways.
Each refers to a _____.
Each has the letter _____ before the final **or**.

3. Look at the other words on the list.
Which two are synonyms?
Which four have double consonants?

Many nouns that refer to a person or occupation end with the letters **tor**:
    doc**tor**   ac**tor**   direc**tor**
Some **or** nouns have a form in which the **o** is accented and easier to hea
    editor—editorial
Mnemonic device: Some **or** words can be remembered by associatio
    other similar **or** words:
    "The **mirror** must be in **error**," said the ugly toad.
    "What is your **favor**ite **flavor**?" asked the ice cream vendor.
    The **horror** film filled us with **terror**.

A All of the spelling words can be used as nouns. Write the singular and plural form of each word.

B Write the **or** words that fit the boxes and clues. Then add **'s** to each word to make a singular possessive phrase.

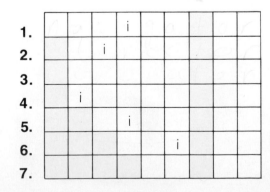

1. _s_ ship

2. _s_ movies

3. _s_ switchboard

4. _____ discovery

5. _____ departure

6. _____ book

7. _____ role

C Make a chart on your paper as shown below. Write each spelling word beside its verb form. If a change is necessary to make the verb a noun, tell what it is in the last column.

Verb Form	Noun Form	Spelling Changes
1. invent	____	____
2. act	____	____
3. operate	____	____
4. edit	____	____
5. color	____	____
6. visit	____	____
7. honor	____	____
8. err	____	____
9. navigate	____	____
10. terrify	____	____
11. equate	____	____
12. doctor	____	____

Build Word Power

The suffixes **able**, **ful**, and **ite** can be added directly to some **or** words to make adjectives. The **or** is changed to **ible** to make some other adjectives.

Dictionary

Write different forms of the same spelling word in each sentence. Use the endings **able**, **ful**, **ite**, **ible**, **s**, and **ed**. Your spelling dictionary will help you find the parts of speech and the spelling of many of the word forms. Some forms may be separate entries.

1. **favor** The ____ (adj.) weather report ____ (v.)

   our trip to my ____ (adj.) island.

2. **honor** The ____ (adj.) guest was ____ (v.) by his country.

3. **color** The child ____ (v.) with ____ (adj.) ____. (n.)

4. **terror** The ____ (adj.) thunder and lightning ____ (v.) everyone.

5. **horror** The ____ (adj.) movie filled the audience with ____. (n.)

navigator   editor   honor   rumor   horror
visitor   director   color   error   equator
doctor   operator   favor   mirror
actor   inventor   flavor   terror

New Words	
author	janitor
aviator	major
governor	sponsor
labored	senator
minor	mayor

Reach Out for New Words

A Use the code to find the new **or** words that fit in this story.

G	W	O	Q	Y	C	N	X	F	M	P	A	R	L
1	2	3	4	5	6	7	8	9	10	11	12	13	14

B	K	S	E	J	U	D	T	I	Z	V	H
15	16	17	18	19	20	21	22	23	24	25	26

The __17 11 3 7 17 3 13 17__ and organizers of the state f... ere

filled with excitement. The __19 12 7 23 22 3 13 17__ and fiel... w had

__14 12 15 3 13 18 21__ for weeks to get the fair grounds rea... the

__10 12 19 3 13__ event of the year. Not a __10 23 7 3 13__ had been

overlooked. Everyone was eager for the fair to begin.

The town __10 12 5 3 13__ introduced the __1 3 25 __ __7 3 13__

of the state and two state __17 18 7 12 22 3 13 17__ w... ded

the opening ceremonies. After the speeches, __12 25 23 __ __3 13 17__ flew

their planes in formation over the marching bands on the ... amous local

__12 20 22 26 3 13__ autographed copies of her book. ...s and

sports heroes returned to their home state for the spec...

Writing

B Seven of the new words refer to people. Write th... ite
a singular possessive phrase with each one.

Writir...

B Write tw...
compou...

The prefix ex

ex + it	=	*exit*
ex + ample	=	*example*
ex + act	=	*exact*
ex + ist	=	*exist*
ex + amine	=	*examine*
ex + ertion	=	*exertion*
ex + aggerate	=	*exaggerate*
ex + hibit	=	*exhibit*
ex + hale	=	*exhale*
ex + haust	=	*exhaust*
ex + claim	=	*exclaim*
ex + ceed	=	*exceed*
ex + cuse	=	*excuse*
ex + ception	=	*exception*
ex + cite	=	*excite*
ex + cellent	=	*excellent*
ex + clamation	=	*exclamation*
ex + cess	=	*excess*

1. In how many words is the **ex** prefix followed by a vowel?
   In how many words is **ex** followed by the letter **h**?   by the letter **c**?

2. Is the **ex** prefix followed by the letter **s** in any of the words?

3. When the prefix and root are joined, do any of the words have a double letter **x**?

> The prefix **ex** never causes any double consonant problems because
>   the letter **x** is never doubled.
> No commonly used words begin with the letters **ex + s**. The
>   letter **x** itself makes the sound of **s** or **z**.
> **Mnemonic device**: **X** marks the spot between the prefix and root.
>   Don't add any <u>ex</u>tra letters!

Practice the Words

A Write the spelling words that complete the puzzle.

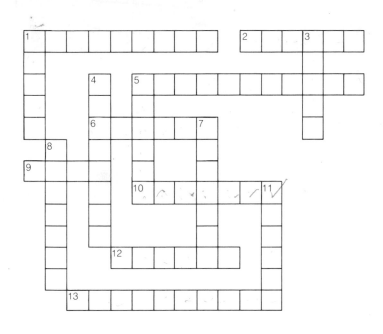

Across

1. not the ordinary
2. too much
5. strong statement
6. pardon; permit to leave
9. leave; go out
10. a sample to follow
12. go beyond a limit
13. overstate the facts

Down

1. accurate
3. be alive
4. the use of effort
5. stir up strong feeling
7. look at closely
8. call out in surprise
11. breathe out

B Make three columns on your paper as shown below. Write the words that begin with these letters.

ex + a vowel	**ex** + **c**	**ex** + **h**
(7 words)	(8 words)	(3 words)

Dictionary

C Find the spelling word that completes both sentences in each pair. Write the sentences. Read the dictionary entry for each spelling word you write. Decide if the word is used as a noun or a verb in each sentence. Write the abbreviation for the part of speech beside the sentence.   *v verb/action*

1. Please ____ me for interrupting. ____

   What was Lyle's ____ for being late? ____

2. Long hikes always ____ me. ____

   Can you smell the ____ from the engine? ____

3. Which way is the ____ ? ____

   The class should ____ quietly during a fire drill. ____

4. The artist will ____ her paintings this weekend. ____

   Did you see the space ____ at the museum? ____

Build Word Power

Change the form of spelling words. Write the form of each underlined word that is needed to make the sentence correct. Then tell what changes you made in spelling. Use your dictionary to help you.

1. The bobsled ride was <u>excite</u>.   Dropped __   Added __
2. All kindergarten children were given an eye <u>examine</u>.   Dropped __   Added __
3. Marla <u>exertion</u> great effort to lift the large box.   Dropped __   Added __
4. Bob's story was an obvious <u>exaggerate</u>.   Dropped __   Added __
5. Tricia's gift was <u>exact</u> what I wanted for my birthday.   Dropped __   Added __
6. The long-distance runner suffered from <u>exhaust</u>.   Dropped __   Added __
7. Inhalation is the opposite of <u>exhale</u>.   Dropped __   Added __
8. Dinosaurs are no longer in <u>exist</u>.   Dropped __   Added __
9. Todd received an award for <u>excellent</u>.   Dropped __   Added __

136

exit	examine	exhale	excuse	exclamation
example	exertion	exhaust	exception	excess
exact	exaggerate	exclaim	excite	
exist	exhibit	exceed	excellent	

New Words
Discover
new words
below!

Reach Out for New Words

A Build two word pyramids using the codes.

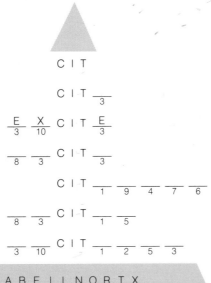

CIT

CIT $\frac{}{3}$

$\frac{E}{3}$ $\frac{X}{10}$ CIT $\frac{E}{3}$

$\frac{}{8}$ $\frac{}{3}$ CIT $\frac{}{3}$

CIT $\frac{}{1}$ $\frac{}{9}$ $\frac{}{4}$ $\frac{}{7}$ $\frac{}{6}$

$\frac{}{8}$ $\frac{}{3}$ CIT $\frac{}{1}$ $\frac{}{5}$

$\frac{}{3}$ $\frac{}{10}$ CIT $\frac{}{1}$ $\frac{}{2}$ $\frac{}{5}$ $\frac{}{3}$

A B E I L N O R T X
1 2 3 4 5 6 7 8 9 10

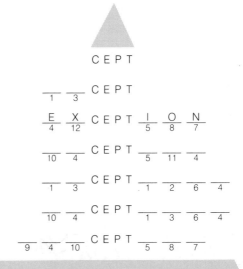

CEPT

$\frac{}{1}$ $\frac{}{3}$ CEPT

$\frac{E}{4}$ $\frac{X}{12}$ CEPT $\frac{I}{5}$ $\frac{O}{8}$ $\frac{N}{7}$

$\frac{}{10}$ $\frac{}{4}$ CEPT $\frac{}{5}$ $\frac{}{11}$ $\frac{}{4}$

$\frac{}{1}$ $\frac{}{3}$ CEPT $\frac{}{1}$ $\frac{}{2}$ $\frac{}{6}$ $\frac{}{4}$

$\frac{}{10}$ $\frac{}{4}$ CEPT $\frac{}{1}$ $\frac{}{3}$ $\frac{}{6}$ $\frac{}{4}$

$\frac{}{9}$ $\frac{}{4}$ $\frac{}{10}$ CEPT $\frac{}{5}$ $\frac{}{8}$ $\frac{}{7}$

A B C E I L N O P R V X
1 2 3 4 5 6 7 8 9 10 11 12

Dictionary

B Look up each pyramid word in your spelling dictionary to find the part of speech. Write each word in the correct column.

Verbs
(4 words)

Nouns
(5 words)

Adjectives
(3 words)

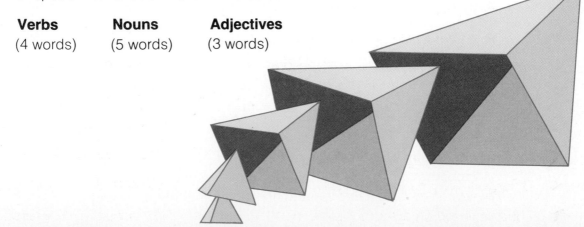

137

More prefix forms

immediately   *opposite*
immigrant   *opponent*
immune   *opportunity*
impossible   *opposed*
impolite
impractical   *appointment*
                     appearance
supplement   *appreciation*
supposed   *applauded*
support
supplied

in = "toward" or "not"	**sub** = "under"
ob = "against" or "before"	**ad** = "toward"

1. Look at the four different prefixes listed in the oval under the spelling list. These prefixes have been used to form the spelling words in this lesson. Do any of the prefixes in the oval end with the letter **m** or the letter **p**?

2. Look at the words formed when the prefixes are added.
   How does the prefix **in** change?   How does the prefix **ob** change?
   How does the prefix **sub** change?   How does the prefix **ad** change?

3. Look at the roots and base words. Do all of them begin with an **m** or a **p**?

4. What spelling problem is caused by some of these changes?

The last letter of a prefix may change to blend more easily with the first letter of a base word or root.

       opposite is easier to say than **obposite**

       appearance is easier to say than **adpearance**

The change often results in a double consonant that may cause spelling problems.

Practice the Words

A Complete the sentences with spelling words.

1. **Tall** is the ____ of **short**.
2. Talking with food in your mouth is ____.
3. Julie's ____ with the dentist is at three o'clock.
4. We gave Kerry a gift to show our ____.
5. My grandmother was an ____ from Spain.
6. My parents are not sure which candidate to ____ in the election.
7. The ambulance responded ____ to the emergency call.
8. Dr. Clark said the shots would make me ____ to polio.
9. We were ____ to go on a field trip, but the bus broke down.
10. The blizzard made it ____ to travel.
11. Larry's idea was interesting, but too ____ to take seriously.
12. The reporters will be given an ____ to ask questions.
13. My ____ beat me by a score of 5 to 3.
14. Jack was nervous before his ____ on stage.
15. I take vitamins to ____ my regular diet.
16. The audience ____ after each act.
17. Some voters are ____ to changing the law.
18. The coach ____ the team with uniforms and equipment.

B Find the misspelled word in each group. Write it correctly.

1. impossible
   suplied
   supposed
   supplement

2. opportunity
   appointment
   impolite
   oposite

3. imigrant
   impractical
   support
   appreciation

4. immune
   impolite
   apreciation
   opportunity

5. inpossible
   immigrant
   opposite
   support

6. appearance
   opponent
   immediately
   suposed

C Add the missing letters. Write each word.

1. a __ p __ i __ t __ e __ t
2. i __ p __ a __ t __ c __ l
3. s __ p __ o __ e __
4. a __ p __ e __ i __ t __ __
5. o __ p __ r __ u __ i __ y
6. i __ m __ d __ a __ e __ y
7. a __ p __ a __ d __ d

8. o __ p __ s __ t __
9. s __ p __ l __ m __ n __
10. a __ p __ a __ a __ c __
11. i __ m __ n __
12. o __ p __ n __ n __
13. i __ p __ l __ t __
14. o __ p __ s __ d

Build Word Power

Write the base form of the spelling words. Then write the words formed by adding these endings to the base words.

1. supposed   = ____ + ing = ____
2. impolite   = ____ + ly = ____
3. opposite   = ____ + ing = ____
4. appreciation = ____ + ed = ____
5. impractical = ____ + ly = ____
6. appearance   = ____ + ing = ____

immediately   impolite   support   opportunity   appreciation
immigrant   impractical supplied   opposed   applauded
immune   supplement   opposite   appointment
impossible   supposed   opponent   appearance

> **New Words**
> Discover new words below!

Reach Out for New Words

A Build a word pyramid by following the code. Use your spelling dictionary to find the four pyramid words that match the definitions.

The root **med** means "middle."

1. refers to the Middle Ages

2. someone in the middle who settles a problem

3. someone who always gets in the middle of another's business

4. not in the middle, but right away

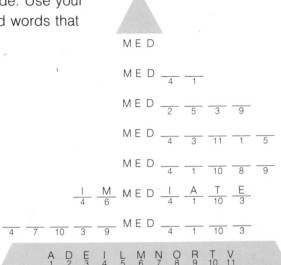

M E D

M E D __ __
     4   1

M E D __ __ __ __
     2 5 3 9

M E D __ __ __ __ __
     4 3 11 1 5

M E D __ __ __ __ __
     4 1 10 8 9

I M MED I A T E
4 6   4 1 10 3

__ __ __ __ __ MED __ __ __ __
4 7 10 3 9   4 1 10 3

A D E I L M N O R T V
1 2 3 4 5 6 7 8 9 10 11

B Build another word pyramid. Use your spelling dictionary to find four pyramid words that match the definitions.

The root **port** means "carry."

1. able to be carried around

2. carried away or out of a place

3. hold up or carry from underneath

4. the system of carrying things from one place to another

P O R T

__ __ PORT __ __
 5 16   5 4

P O R T __ __ __ __
        1 2 7 5

S U P PORT
13 15 11

__ __ PORT __ __ __ __
 6 8   1 9 3 5

O P PORT U N I T Y
10 11   15 9 6 14 17

__ __ __ __ __ PORT __ __ __ __ __
14 12 1 9 13   1 14 6 10 9

A B C D E I L M N O P R S T U X Y
1 2 3 4 5 6 7 8 9 10 11 12 13 14 15 16 17

141

hydrant
cyclone
style
hyphen
bicycle
typing
encyclopedia
gypsy
system
antonym
syllable
pyramid
myth
crystal
symptom
typhoon
python
paralyze

1. Where is the letter **y** in most familiar words, such as **my**, **why**, and **story**?
2. Where is the letter **y** in some words, such as **nylon** and **type**?
3. Where is the letter **y** in all of the spelling words?

The letter **y** is often used as **i** in words taken from the Greek language. It is used within the word as a vowel. It may be pronounced as a long or a short vowel: **style   myth**

Practice the Words

A Write the list word that fits in each shape.

1.
2. symptom
3.
4.
5.
6. m
7.
8.
9.
10.
11.
12.
13.
14.

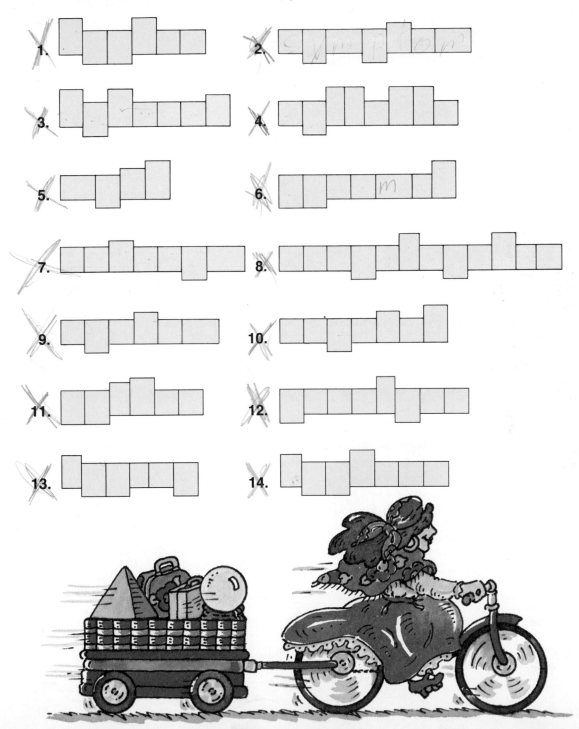

B **1.** Write five list words that end with a final silent **e**.

2. One list word is a final silent **e** word + suffix. Remove the suffix and write the base form.

3. Write the plural form of the final **y** word.

C The letter **y** acts like a vowel in these words. Complete the words by adding the missing **y** or vowel that fits in each space. Write each word.

1. t __ p __ n g
2. s t __ l __
3. s __ s t __ m
4. p __ t h __ n
5. g __ p s __
6. c r __ s t __ l
7. h __ p h __ n
8. h __ d r __ n t
9. __ n c __ c l __ p __ d __ __

10. s __ l l __ b l __
11. b __ c __ c l __
12. p __ r __ m __ d
13. __ n t __ n __ m
14. p __ r __ l __ z __
15. s __ m p t __ m
16. c __ c l __ n __
17. t __ p h __ __ n

Build Word Power

Proofreading

Proofread the following sentences for spelling errors. Find the misspelled words. Rewrite the sentences correctly.

1. I would like to see the gipsy dancers in Spain and the piramyds in Egypt.

2. We learned about using hyphyns between sylables, finding antonyms for words, and locating information in the encyclypedia.

hydrant	bicycle	system	myth	python	
cyclone	typing	antonym	crystal	paralyze	
style	encyclopedia	syllable	symptom		
hyphen	gypsy	pyramid	typhoon		

New Words

cypress	typical
tyrant	lyric
dynamic	dehydrate
hyacinth	hypnotism

3. The cyclone upended the hydrant and smashed the bycycle like a piece of cristal.

4. Brian's typeing speed and well-organized filing systym made him an excellent secretary.

5. The sight of a pithon can paralyse a smaller animal.

Reach Out for New Words

A Look at the eight new **y** words above. They are hidden in two directions in the puzzle. ↓ → Write the word after you have circled it in the puzzle.

```
h a c a t y r a n t
y d e h y d r a t e
p y u v p r o c n p
n n a p i d r s m b
o a r a c w g e t t
t m h y a c i n t h
i i t a l y r i c g
s c y p r e s s o n
m p s r a d y z l y
```

Writing

B Use as many of the words as possible in a brief paragraph about a fictional tropical island. Describe the weather, the plants, the ruler, and the problems on this fantasy island.

145

sign
design
gnat
campaign
foreigner
resigned

spaghetti
ghost

twilight
frightened
thigh
flight
sighed
straight
although
thoughtful
doughnut
ought

1. What letter is silent in the first six words?   What letter follows this silent letter?

2. In the next two words, the letter **g** is pronounced.
   What is the silent letter that follows **g**?

3. What two letters are silent in all of the last ten words?

The letters **g** and **h** are often silent consonants in certain combinations. Learn to recognize the combinations. Invent mnemonic devices for words that are special problems for you.

Practice the Words

A Add the missing silent letters. Write each word.

1. s i ___ n

2. f o r e i ___ n e r

3. ___ n a t

4. s t r a i ___ ___ t

5. s p a g ___ e t t i

6. g ___ o s t

7. f r i ___ ___ t e n e d

8. s i ___ ___ e d

9. d o u ___ ___ n u t

10. f l i ___ ___ t

11. t h o u ___ ___ t f u l

12. c a m p a i ___ n

13. d e s i ___ n

14. t w i l i ___ ___ t

15. a l t h o u ___ ___

16. t h i ___ ___

17. o u ___ ___ t

18. r e s i ___ n e d

B Use the clues to find spelling words.

1. not dawn, but ___

2. not a mosquito, but a ___

3. not arm, but ___

4. not crooked, but ___

5. not lasagna, but ___

6. not a native, but a ___

7. not a random pattern, but a ___

8. not unplanned actions, but a ___

9. not yawned, but ___

10. not careless, but ___

Proofreading

C Find the eight misspelled words in the story. Write each word correctly.

It was twilight when the hungry traveler saw the restaurant sine and sighed with relief. Her last meal had been a single dohnut at breakfast. Happy thoughts of a spegetti dinner gave her the strength to walk down the last block and slowly open the door. Altho she tried to sneak unseen into the dining room, Gertrude immediately heard the usual screams. She quickly took flite, sadly leaving the wonderful smell of spaghetti behind. She wondered why people were always so frigtened by a nice old gost who happened to love spaghetti. They aught to be more considerate!

Build Word Power

A silent letter can regain its sound in some words by changing the form of the word. The silent **g** changes in some forms of words made from the base word **sign**.

1. **sign**   When you sign your name, you write your _____.
                Use your spelling dictionary to divide the word into syllables.
                Mark the accent.

2. **design**   When you point out who is to do something, you _____ a person.
                Divide the word into syllables. Mark the accent.

3. **resign**   When you resign from a job, you give your _____.
                Divide the word into syllables and mark the accent.

In the three new words you have written, what happened to the silent consonant combination **gn**?

In the new word forms, the letter **g** is in one _____.

The letter **n** is in another _____.

When they are separated in this way, both letters are pronounced.

sign	foreigner	twilight	sighed	doughnut
design	resigned	frightened	straight	ought
gnat	spaghetti	thigh	although	
campaign	ghost	flight	thoughtful	

New Words

gnash	gnaw
almighty	knighthood
highlands	ghastly
gnu	

Reach Out for New Words

A Find the seven new words in the puzzle. Then write each word.
Circle the silent letter or letters in each word you write.

B Complete the story with forms of your seven new words.

Corey of Gnuland had always wanted to be a knight. To prove

his bravery, he decided to journey to the ＿＿ of Gnuland.

There he would battle the ＿＿ ogres that were attacking the

helpless ＿＿ who lived there. Corey faced the huge monsters who

growled at him and ＿＿ their teeth that they sharpened by ＿＿

on tree trunks. Corey closed his eyes and asked the ＿＿

powers for strength. Then he fought the ogres—and won! He returned

home, and that very day he was welcomed into the ＿＿ by

the Royal Grand Gnu himself!

28
autobiography
television
symphony

29
it is
they are
would have

it's
they're
would've
typewriter
forty-two

30
visitor
operator
flavor
error

31
exist
exaggerate
excite
excuse

32
immediately
supposed
opposite

33
bicycle
encyclopedia
style

34
thoughtful
straight
frightened

A Complete each analogy with the correct form of a spelling word.

1. **acted** is to **actor** as **erred** is to ____
2. **styling** is to **styled** as **supposing** is to ____
3. **flavor** is to **flavorful** as **thought** is to ____
4. **navigate** is to **navigator** as **operate** is to ____
5. **exciting** is to **excite** as **excusing** is to ____
6. **frighten** is to **fright** as **straighten** is to ____
7. **examination** is to **examine** as **exaggeration** is to ____
8. **appointment** is to **appoint** as **excitement** is to ____
9. **we are** is to **we're** as **they are** is to ____
10. **impolite** is to **impolitely** as **immediate** is to ____
11. **straighten** is to **straightened** as **frighten** is to ____
12. **telescopes** is to **telescope** as **typewriters** is to ____
13. **who is** is to **who's** as **it is** is to ____
14. **automobiles** is to **automobile** as **bicycles** is to ____
15. **you're** is to **you are** as **they're** is to ____

B Use spelling words to complete the story.

My brother and I were watching an exciting ____ show about a well-known person, and wondering what it would be like to be famous. Sean said that by the time he was ____ years old, he would be so famous he would write his ____. He said people would ask for his autograph and copy the ____ of his clothes.

"____ me," I said, "but what will you do to become so famous?"

"____ easy," he replied. "I'll invent a brand new ice cream ____ that no one will be able to resist. I'll call it . . . ."

What do you think Sean will call his new ice cream flavor? Can you make up a name for it?

C Find the one misspelled word in each group. Write it correctly.

1. typewriter
enciclopedia
operator
thoughtful

2. exsist
error
supposed
straight

3. immediately
frightened
forty-two
would'of

4. they're
flavor
excite
oposite

5. excuse
visiter
it's
style

6. television
autobiography
simphony
exaggerate

Using More Review Words

A Follow the directions to make related forms of spelling words.

1. bicycle	minus **bi**	plus **tri**	=	_____
2. exhibit	minus **ex**	plus **in**	=	_____
3. opposite	minus **op**	plus **com**	=	_____
4. immigrant	minus **ant**	plus **ation**	=	_____
5. immune		plus **ity**	=	_____
6. exhibit		plus **ion**	=	_____
7. supposed	minus **sup**	plus **pro**	=	_____
8. appreciation	minus **ap**	plus **de**	=	_____
9. system		plus **atic**	=	_____
10. exhale	minus **ex**	plus **in**	=	_____
11. antonym	minus **ant**	plus **hom**	=	_____
12. terror	minus **or**	plus **ible**	=	_____
13. horror	minus **or**	plus **ible**	=	_____
14. editor		plus **ial**	=	_____
15. director	minus **or**	plus **ion**	=	_____

B Three words in each row follow the same spelling pattern. Write the word that does not follow the same pattern. Be ready to tell why it does not belong.

1. typewriter   phonograph   roommate   nighttime
2. foreigner   inventor   visitor   director
3. syllable   system   biography   myth
4. spaghetti   ghost   although   exhale
5. autograph   earthquake   geography   telephone
6. editor   example   exhibit   exclaim
7. immune   support   exception   appearance
8. campaign   design   gnat   gypsy

C Complete each analogy with a spelling word from the box.

> 7 hydrant   12 gnat   8 television   10 three-fourths
> 6 spaghetti 1 nighttime 2 syllable   4 typewriter
> 3 flavor   5 bicycle   13 geography   14 pyramids
> 11 cyclone   9 hyphen   15 sympathy

1. **dawn** is to **daytime** as **twilight** is to _____
2. **sentence** is to **word** as **word** is to _____
3. **red** is to **color** as **chocolate** is to _____
4. **feet** is to **bicycle** as **fingers** is to _____
5. **keys** is to **typewriter** as **pedals** is to _____
6. **ham** is to **eggs** as **meatballs** is to _____
7. **gas** is to **pump** as **water** is to _____
8. **hear** is to **telephone** as **see** is to _____
9. **contraction** is to **apostrophe** as **compound** is to _____
10. **two-fourths** is to **one-half** as **six-eighths** is to _____
11. **tremor** is to **earthquake** as **wind** is to _____
12. **food** is to **spaghetti** as **bug** is to _____
13. **life** is to **biography** as **earth** is to _____
14. **England** is to **castles** as **Egypt** is to _____
15. **sound** is to **symphony** as **feeling** is to _____

SPELLING AND THE PROCESS OF WRITING

career	daily	grateful	diploma
reward	folks	talent	routine
seemed	rich	lifetime	letting
skills	bank	purpose	among
most	pride	training	brain

Prewriting. Prewriting is the thinking and planning you do before you begin to write. In this lesson, you will plan and write a **paragraph that explains why**. You will write about what you want to be someday, and you will give reasons for your choice.

Use Prewriting Skills

A Answer the questions with spelling words. These words will give you ideas for writing about careers.

1. What do you receive when you graduate from high school or college?

2. What do you use to think and solve problems in a job?

3. What do you develop as you work in a job?

4. What are you doing when you are learning a job?

5. What word means the activities you do daily?

6. What word means your aim or goal in life?

7. What word means the feeling you have for a job well done?

8. What do you call a natural ability to perform a certain skill?

9. What word means the prize for a job well done?

10. What two words refer to lengths of time on a job?

11. Where would you go to get a loan for a business?

12. What three words could you substitute for the underlined words in this sentence? The student <u>appeared</u> <u>very</u> <u>thankful</u> for the chance to develop her talent.

B Plan to begin your paragraph with a topic sentence that states your main idea. Your main idea should be narrow enough to be developed in one paragraph. Write the main idea that has been narrowed in each pair.

1. career in dentistry
career as a dental hygienist

2. becoming an entertainer
developing the talent of singing

3. practicing a craft
learning the skill of woodworking

4. training to be a doctor
training to be a brain surgeon

5. leading a daily exercise class
promoting physical fitness

6. handling animals
working among circus elephants

C Plan at least three good reasons to support your main idea. Make sure your reasons relate to your topic.

Read the main idea and list of reasons below. Choose and write the three reasons that best support and relate to the main idea. Often, you will order these ideas from least important to most important.

Main Idea. Why I would choose a career as a bank teller

enjoy helping folks handle money
prefer taking a bus to a daily job
would be letting me operate a computer
seems a rich opportunity for using my math skills
have no talent for singing or acting

Now Think Make prewriting notes about a career you might choose someday. Write your main idea. Make sure you have narrowed it enough. Then list reasons to tell why you chose that career. Number your reasons in order from the least important to the most important.

Writing. When you write a paragraph that explains why, you must give reasons that are clearly stated. When stating reasons, you can combine sentences with **because** or **since** to make the reasons clearer.

> Example: I want to be well prepared. (because)
> I like to take pride in my work.
> I want to be well prepared because I like to take pride in my work.

Sometimes the reason is given first. Then a comma is placed after it.
> Example: Because I like to take pride in my work, I want to be well prepared.

Use Writing Skills

Combine each pair of sentences with the word in parentheses. If the word comes first, begin the sentence with it and use a comma after the reason.

1. I plan to go to college. (since)
A diploma is necessary for my career.

2. Dad is letting me use his typewriter. (because)
I hope to become a secretary.

3. (since) My favorite place is the sea.
I'm going to study ocean life.

4. Factory work would suit me. (because)
I like to follow a regular routine.

5. (because) I like to be among animals.
It would be fun to work in a zoo.

6. (because) I want to go into athletics.
I work out daily in a gym.

Now Write

Look over your prewriting notes. Use them to write a first draft of your paragraph about a career. Begin with a topic sentence that names the career. Give a few details about the career. Then give three or more reasons for your choice. State the reasons from the least important to the most important.

Revising. When you revise a paragraph that explains why, you can add details to make your sentences more specific.

Use Revising Skills

A Make each sentence more specific by adding the words in parentheses.

> Example: A bank teller is responsible for keeping track of money. (careful, large sums)
> A bank teller is responsible for keeping <u>careful</u> track of <u>large</u> <u>sums</u> of money.

1. Playing music seems to calm patients in a dental office. (soft, nervous)

2. One purpose of a recreation worker is to help people use their time well. (vacationing, leisure)

3. Seeing many customers is the salesperson's reward. (satisfied, successful)

4. Planning programs is part of a librarian's routine. (cultural, daily)

B Proofread this set of reasons from an explanatory paragraph. Find the mistakes in capitalization, punctuation, and spelling. Then write the reasons correctly.

Remember
- Do not use a comma after **because** or **since**.
- Do not capitalize occupations unless they are used in titles.
- Use an apostrophe in a contraction.

The career of Hairdressing appeals to me because, I can complete the training and earn a diploma in less than two years. Also, Ive already saved enough money for tuition, Amung the other reasens for my choice is the fact that this job never seems too rutine.

C Revise the following first draft. The directions below will help you. Then make a corrected copy on your own paper.

1. Find one reason that is not a good one.
2. Find two sentences that need to be combined with **because** or **since**.
3. Insert the word **precious** in line 6, and **ancient** in line 11.
4. Find six misspelled words. Write them correctly.
5. Correct the capitalization errors in lines 5 and 11.
6. Correct the punctuation errors in lines 8 and 12.

1   When I grow up, I would like to become an archaeologist. An archaeologist

2   is a scientist who studies the ruins of ancient societies. The perpose is to

3   understand the life and culture of these societies. Archaeologists sometimes

4   acquire several deplomas. Since they must study history, languages, and

5   several sciences. some archaeologists use their skils working outdoors. Others

6   use their talents working among artifacts in museums. I would like to be an

7   archaeologist. I would like to travel to foriegn countries. Another reason this

8   carear appeals to me is, because I have had some training in dating the ages

9   of trees and arrow heads. I like this career because being a lawyer doesn't

10   appeal to me. Most of all, I like the idea of using my brain to solve mysteries. As

11   an Archaeologist, I would be a prehystoric detective. What secrets I might

12   uncover?

Now Revise

Read the first draft of your own paragraph about a career. Have you given some details about the career? Have you stated at least three reasons for your choice? Did you list the reasons in order from the least to the most important? Did you combine any sentences with **because** or **since**? Now proofread for mistakes in grammar, capitalization, punctuation, and spelling. Make a final copy in your best handwriting.

Read your paragraph to others. They will enjoy hearing how you have used the process of writing to explain why a certain career is interesting to you.

Handbook

I The Structure of Words

Syllables
Base Words
Roots
Prefixes
Suffixes
Contractions
Compound Words
Abbreviations

II The Function of Words

Nouns
Possessive Forms
Verbs
Adjectives
Adverbs

III The Sound of Words

Vowels
Indistinct Vowels
Consonants
Silent Letters
Stressed and Unstressed Syllables

I **The Structure of Words** means the way words are put together.

Syllables

Words are made up of parts called syllables. The dictionary shows how words are divided into syllables.

but·ter = two syllables
dress = one syllable

Base Words

Base words are words before any changes have been made.

Base word	wrap
Base word with endings added	wrap<u>s</u> wrap<u>ped</u> wrap<u>ping</u>
Base word with prefix added	<u>un</u>wrap

Roots

Roots are word parts that cannot stand alone. They grow into words when they are joined to prefixes or suffixes.

pend (root meaning "to hang")
<u>de</u>pend (root + prefix)
pend<u>ent</u> (root + suffix)
<u>de</u>pend<u>ent</u> (root + prefix *and* suffix)

Prefixes

A prefix is a group of letters added to the beginning of a word or root to change the meaning. For example, **pre** is a prefix meaning "before." Therefore, the word **prefix** literally means "to fix before."

The word **informed** means "having information or news."

1. He was an <u>informed</u> speaker.
   (He knew what he was talking about.)
2. He was a <u>misinformed</u> speaker.
   (He had wrong or incorrect information.)
3. He was an <u>uninformed</u> speaker.
   (He had no information.)

Suffixes

A suffix is an ending added to a word or root to change the way it is used in a sentence. The meaning of the root or base word does not change.

inform	to give knowledge or news (verb)
informer	one who gives news (noun)
information	news (noun)
informative	providing news (adjective)

The base word **inform** keeps its basic meaning in all these forms. Its *use* changes from verb to noun to adjective.

Common Noun Suffixes

ment	tion	ness	ity	ence	er	ian
	ion		ty	ance	ar	ist
	sion		y		or	
	ation					

Common Verb Suffixes

ify	ize	ate	ish	en
	ise			

Common Adjective Suffixes

ly	ous	ful	ive	al	able	ate	ar	ery
	ious			ial	ible		iar	ary
	eous							ory

Common Adverb Suffixes

ly	ily

Contractions

A contraction is made from two words. When two words are put together, an apostrophe takes the place of one or more letters.

we are = we **a**re = we're   he will = he **wi**ll = he'll

Compound Words

A compound word is made from two smaller words. The spellings
do not change when the words are put together.

class + room = classroom   after + noon = afternoon

Sometimes the words are joined with a hyphen.

three + fourths = three-fourths   cross + country = cross-country

Abbreviations

An abbreviation is a shortened form of a word.
Abbreviations may use the first few letters of a word followed by a period.

Days:	Tuesday-Tues.	Wednesday-Wed.
Months:	December-Dec.	September-Sept.
Titles:	Reverend-Rev.	Captain-Capt.
Addresses:	Avenue-Ave.	Street-St.
Businesses:	Company-Co.	Incorporated-Inc.
Measurements:	inch-in.	dozen-doz.
Parts of Speech:	noun-n.	adverb-adv.

Abbreviations may use the first and last letter of a word followed by a period.

Mister-Mr.   foot-ft.   Road-Rd.   Doctor-Dr.   yard-yd.   hour-hr.

Abbreviations may use all capital letters without periods.

Maryland-MD   New York-NY   California-CA

Abbreviations may use all capital letters with periods.

Doctor of Medicine-M.D.   Registered Nurse-R.N.

A few common abbreviations do not follow any of these patterns.

ounce-oz.   pound-lb.   manager-mgr.
Ms. may be used for either married or unmarried women instead
of Miss or Mrs.

The Function of Words means the way words are used.

Nouns

A noun is a word that names something. A noun that names one thing is called a singular noun. A noun that names more than one thing is a plural noun.

The <u>monkey</u> ate a <u>banana</u>.   The <u>monkeys</u> ate some <u>bananas</u>.
(Two singular nouns)   (Two plural nouns)

Possessive Forms

The possessive form of a noun shows that something belongs to someone. Make the possessive form of a singular noun by adding **'s**.

That car belongs to my father.
That is my <u>father's</u> car.

When a plural noun ends in **s**, add only an apostrophe to make the possessive form.

Those uniforms belong to the players.
Those are the <u>players'</u> uniforms.

When a plural noun does *not* end in **s**, add **'s** to make the possessive form.

These toys belong to the children.
These are the <u>children's</u> toys.

A possessive pronoun takes the place of a noun in the possessive form.

My <u>father's</u> car = <u>his</u> car
The <u>Clark's</u> house = <u>their</u> house
<u>Ashley's</u> book = <u>her</u> book

A possessive pronoun is *not* spelled with an apostrophe.

Verbs

A verb is a word that tells about an action. The ending may change to tell when the action happened.

I <u>walk</u> on the beach in the summertime. (present tense)
We <u>walked</u> a mile to the beach. (past tense)
We are <u>walking</u> to the beach. (present participle)

Adjectives

An adjective is a word that describes something.

We walked along the <u>sandy</u> shore.
(<u>Sandy</u> describes the shore.)

This is my <u>favorite</u> song.
(<u>Favorite</u> describes the song.)

Adverbs

An adverb is a word that tells <u>how</u> or <u>how much</u>.

The sailor acted <u>bravely</u> during the storm.
(<u>Bravely</u> tells how the sailor acted.)

III The Sound of Words means the way you say words when you speak. Sometimes the sound will help you to spell a word.

Vowels

Five letters of the alphabet are called vowels. The vowels are **a**, **e**, **i**, **o**, and **u**.

Indistinct Vowels

Indistinct vowels are vowels that are difficult to hear or identify.

begg_r (The missing vowel could be **e** or **a**.)
ben_fit (The missing vowel could be **i**, **e**, **u**, or **a**.)

Consonants

The consonants are all the letters of the alphabet except **a**, **e**, **i**, **o**, and **u**.

Silent Letters

Silent letters make no sound. You can see them in a word, but you cannot hear them. Silent letters may appear at the beginning, in the middle, or at the end of words.

knee   straight   autumn
wrist   doubt   amaze
gnat   talk   thumb

Stressed and Unstressed Syllables

Stress is the amount of emphasis placed on a syllable when you pronounce a word. The accent mark in a dictionary shows you which syllable receives the most stress.

man′   The one syllable is stressed.
be·gin′   The second syllable is stressed.

Unstressed syllables cause spelling problems because they are hard to hear and likely to be pronounced carelessly.

gram′ mar (the last syllable is often slurred)
vic′ to·ry (often pronounced *vic-try*)

The more stress there is on a syllable, the more clearly it is heard and the easier it is to spell. Sometimes the unstressed syllable is stressed in a related form of the same word.

gram′ mar   gram·ma′ ti·cal
vic′ to·ry   vic·tor′ i·ous

The indistinct vowels **a** and **o** are no longer indistinct when they are in accented syllables.

How To Use a Dictionary

How To Find a Word

A dictionary is organized like a telephone book. It lists information in alphabetical order with guide words at the top of each page.

Guide Words

The guide words help you find the right page quickly. They tell you at a glance what section of the alphabet is included on each page. The guide word on the left tells you the first word on that page. The guide word on the right tells you the last word on that page. If the word you are looking for comes alphabetically between those two words, you are on the right page.

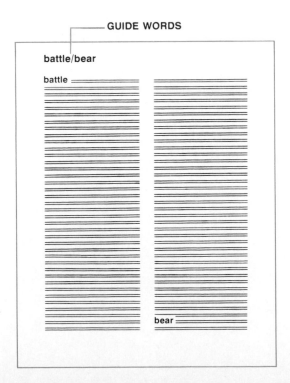

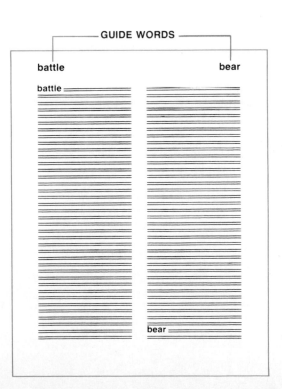

Alphabetical Order

Alphabetical order means the order of the letters in the alphabet.

Words beginning with **a** come first.   **a**bout

Words beginning with **b** come next.   **b**ear

Words beginning with **c** come   **c**lass
after words beginning with **b**.

When two words begin with the same letter, you must look at the second letter of each word to determine alphabetical order. When several of the letters are the same, you will have to look at the third or fourth letter to determine the alphabetical order.

toa**d**   The first three letters in the words <u>toad</u> and <u>toast</u>

toa**st**   are the same. The fourth letter must be used to determine alphabetical order. Since **d** comes before **s**, <u>toad</u> is alphabetized before <u>toast</u>.

What the Dictionary Tells About a Word

A dictionary tells you much more than the spelling and meaning of a word. The information it contains about each word is called the entry. The parts of an entry are labeled and explained below.

The ENTRY WORD is printed in heavy black type. It is divided into syllables.

The DEFINITION is the meaning of the word. If a word has more than one meaning, each meaning is given a number.

An ETYMOLOGY, or word history, may be shown in a special note at the end of an entry.

The PART OF SPEECH is shown as an abbreviation after the pronunciation. Some words may have more than one part of speech.

A sample SENTENCE OR PHRASE can help you understand the meaning of the entry word.

The RESPELLING tells you how to pronounce the word. The *Pronunciation Key* explains the respelling.

A PICTURE may be used to help you understand the meaning of the entry word.

OTHER FORMS of the entry word are included in the same entry.

A STRESS MARK is placed after a syllable that gets an accent.

glimpse (glimps) ***v.*** to get a quick look at [I *glimpsed* a fox as it ran across the trail.] —**glimpsed, glimps′ ing** •***n.*** a quick look.

glo·ri·ous (glôr′ ē əs) ***adj.*** giving, having, or deserving glory or honor [a *glorious* act of bravery].

glos·sa·ry (gläs′ ə rē *or* glôs′ ə rē) ***n.*** a list of hard words with their meanings. —*pl.* **glos′ sa·ries**

Glossary comes from a Greek word meaning "tongue." Since the tongue is so important in forming words, it is easy to see the connection between the old Greek word and our modern term for a list of words.

gnash (nash) ***v.*** to grind the teeth together, as in anger or pain.

gnat (nat) ***n.*** a small insect that bites or stings.

gnaw (nô) ***v.*** to bite and wear away bit by bit with the teeth [The dog *gnawed* on the bone.]

gnu (no͞o *or* nyo͞o) ***n.*** a large African antelope.

gor·geous (gôr′ jəs) ***adj.*** magnificent [The tail of a peacock is *gorgeous*.] —**gor′ geous·ly** ***adv.***

gov·er·nor (guv′ ər nər) ***n.*** the person elected head of a state of the United States.

Dictionary

SYMBOL	KEY WORDS	SYMBOL	KEY WORDS	SYMBOL	KEY WORDS
a	ask, fat	u	up, cut	n	not, ton
ā	ape, date	ʉr	fur, fern	p	put, tap
ä	car, lot			r	red, dear
		ə	a in ago	s	sell, pass
e	elf, ten		e in agent	t	top, hat
er	berry, care		e in father	v	vat, have
ē	even, meet		i in unity	w	will, always
			o in collect	y	yet, yard
i	is, hit		u in focus	z	zebra, haze
ir	mirror, here				
ī	ice, fire			ch	chin, arch
		b	bed, dub	ng	ring, singer
ō	open, go	d	did, had	sh	she, dash
ô	law, horn	f	fall, off	th	thin, truth
oi	oil, point	g	get, dog	th	then, father
oo	look, pull	h	he, ahead	zh	s in pleasure
ōō	ooze, tool	j	joy, jump		
yoo	unite, cure	k	kill, bake	'	as in (āʹbʹl)
yōō	cute, few	l	let, ball		
ou	out, crowd	m	met, trim		

A heavy stress mark ʹ is placed after a syllable that gets a strong accent, as in **con·sid·er** (kən sidʹər).

A light stress mark ʹ is placed after a syllable that also gets an accent, but of a weaker kind, as in **dic·tion·ar·y** (dikʹshən erʹē).

The following abbreviations are used in your dictionary for part of speech labels. They are usually shown in dark italic type.

n.	noun	*pron.*	pronoun	*adv.*	adverb	*conj.*	conjunction
v.	verb	*adj.*	adjective	*prep.*	preposition	*interj.*	interjection

The dictionary definitions used throughout this book were specially prepared by the staff of McDougal, Littell & Company and are based upon the entries in *Webster's New World Dictionary for Young Readers* with the consent of the publisher of that work, Simon & Schuster, Inc.

A

-a·ble (ə b'l) *a suffix meaning* able to be; that can be [A *drinkable* liquid is one that can be drunk.]

ac·cent (ak′ sent) *n.* **1** extra stress given to some syllables or words in speaking [The *accent* in "accident" is on the first syllable.] **2** the way of pronouncing used by people from a certain region or country [My mother speaks with an Irish *accent.*]

ac·cen·ted (ak′ sen·təd) *adj.* stressed.

ac·cept (ək sept′) *v.* to take what is offered or given [Will you *accept* $20 for that old bicycle?]

ac·cept·a·ble (ək sep′ tə b'l) *adj.* good enough; satisfactory [an *acceptable* answer]. —**ac·cept′ a·bly** *adv.*

ac·ci·dent (ak′ sə dent) *n.* an unfortunate happening that causes damage [I've had three *accidents* driving a car.]

ac·ci·den·tal (ak′ sə den′ t'l) *adj.* happening by chance —**ac′ ci·den′ tal·ly** *adv.*

ac·com·plished (ə käm′ plisht) *adj.* done; completed [an *accomplished* project].

ac·com·plish·ment (ə käm′ plish mənt) *n.* a task successfully completed [Digging the Panama Canal was a great *accomplishment.*]

ac·cuse (ə kyo͞oz′) *v.* to find fault with; blame [They *accused* her of being lazy.]

ache (āk) *v.* to have or give a dull, steady pain [My head *aches.*] —**ached, ach′ ing** ♦*n.* a dull, steady pain.

ac·quit (ə kwit′) *v.* to rule that a person is not guilty [The judge *acquitted* the suspect.] —**ac·quit′ ted, ac·quit′ ting**

act (akt) *v.* **1** to play the part of [She *acted* Juliet.] **2** to do something [We must *act* now.]

ac·tor (ak′ tər) *n.* a person who acts in plays, movies, etc.

ac·tu·al·ly (ak′ choo wəl ē *or* ak′ chə lē) *adv.* really; in fact [We *actually* had no money.]

ad- (ad, əd, id) *a prefix meaning* toward, of, nearness to.

ad·di·tion (ə dish′ ən) *n.* **1** an adding of numbers to get a sum. **2** a joining of one thing to another [The lemonade was improved by the *addition* of sugar.]

ad·di·tion·al (ə dish′ ən əl) *adj.* more; extra [We ordered an *additional* supply of pencils.] —**ad·di·′ tion·al·ly** *adv.*

ad·dress (ə dres′) *v.* to write on a letter or package the name, street number, city, etc. of the one to whom it is being sent. ♦*n.* (ə dres′ *or* ad′ res) the place to which mail or goods can be sent.

ad·he·sive (əd hēs′ iv) *n.* a sticky substance [Glue is an *adhesive.*]

ad·jec·tive (aj′ ik tiv) *n.* a word used with a noun or pronoun to tell which, what kind, how many, or whose. —**ad·jec·ti′ val** (aj′ ik tī′ v'l) *adj.*

a	fat	ir	here	ou	out	zh	leisure
ā	ape	ī	bite, fire	u	up	ng	ring
ä	car, lot	ō	go	ur	fur		a *in* ago
e	ten	ô	law, horn	ch	chin		e *in* agent
er	care	oi	oil	sh	she	ə =	i *in* unity
ē	even	oo	look	th	thin		o *in* collect
i	hit	oo	tool	th	then		u *in* focus

ad·mi·ra·ble (ad′ mər ə b'l) *adj.* deserving to be admired or praised; excellent [an *admirable* student]. —**ad′ mi·ra·bly** *adv.*

ad·mis·sion (əd mish′ ən) *n.* **1** the right of entering [The reporter was refused *admission* to the meeting.] **2** the price paid for entering [*Admission* to the movie was three dollars.]

ad·mit (əd mit′) *v.* to permit or give the right to enter [One ticket *admits* two persons.] —**ad·mit′ ted, ad·mit′ ting**

a·dopt (ə däpt′) *v.* to take into one's family by a legal process [They *adopted* their daughter when she was four months old.]

a·dor·a·ble (ə dôr′ ə b'l) *adj.* very attractive; delightful; charming [What an *adorable* cottage!]

a·dult (ə dult′ *or* ad′ ult) *adj.* grown up [He is an *adult* person.] ◆*n.* mature person.

ad·vance (əd vans′) *v.* to go or bring forward [On first down they *advanced* the football two yards.] —**ad·vanced′, ad·vanc′ ing**

ad·ven·tur·ous (əd ven′ chər əs) *adj.* willing to take risks [an *adventurous* explorer].

ad·verb (ad′ vərb) *n.* a word used with a verb, adjective, or another adverb to tell when, where, how, what kind, or how much. *Quickly* tells how in "run *quickly*." —**ad·ver·bi·al** (ad vʉr′ bē əl) *adj.*

ad·ver·tise (ad′ vər tīz) *v.* to tell about a product in such a way as to make people want to buy it [to *advertise* cars on television]. —**ad′ ver·tised, ad′ ver·tis·ing** —**ad′ ver tis′ er** *n.*

Advertise comes from a word in Latin which means "to turn to." Advertising is meant to turn our attention to something so that we will want to use or buy it.

---

ad·vice (əd vīs′) *n.* opinion as to what or how to do something [We followed her *advice* in selecting a home.]

a·gainst (ə genst′) *prep.* opposite or opposed to [Vote *against* the bill.]

a·gree·ment (ə grē′ mənt) *n.* the fact of agreeing or being similar [The news report was not in *agreement* with the facts.]

aisle (īl) *n.* an open way between sections of seats, as in a theater.

-al (əl) *a suffix meaning* of, like, or suitable for [*Musical* sounds are sounds of or like music.]

al·ley (al′ ē) *n.* a narrow street between or behind buildings. —*pl.* **al′ leys**

al·low·a·ble (ə lou′ ə b'l) *adj.* that can be allowed; permissible.

al·might·y (ôl mīt′ ē) *adj.* having power with no limit; all-powerful.

al·mond (ä′ mənd *or* am′ ənd) *n.* an oval nut.

al·pha·bet·i·cal (al′ fə bet′i k'l) *adj.* arranged in the order of the alphabet [Entries in a dictionary are in *alphabetical* order.] —**al′ pha·bet′ i·cal·ly** *adv.*

al·tar (ôl′ tər) *n.* a table used for religious rituals [The groom stood before the *altar*.]

al·though (ôl thō′) *conj.* in spite of the fact that [*Although* the sun is shining, it may rain later.]

a·maze (ə māz′) *v.* to cause to feel surprise or wonder [They were *amazed* at the great height of the waterfall.] —**a·mazed′, a·maz′ ing**

a·maze·ment (ə māz′ ment) *n.* great surprise or wonder.

a·mong (ə mung′) *prep.* **1** in the company of [You are *among* friends.] **2** from place to place in [They passed *among* the crowd.] **3** with a share for each of [The estate was divided *among* the relatives.] **4** with one another [Don't quarrel *among* yourselves.]

an·chor (ang′ kər) *n.* a heavy object let down into the water by a chain to keep a ship from drifting.

an·gel (ān′ j'l) *n.* a being that is supposed to live in heaven and have more power and goodness than human beings.

an·gle (ang′ g'l) *n.* **1** the shape made by two straight lines meeting in a point. **2** the space between such lines or surfaces. It is measured in degrees.

an·ni·ver·sa·ry (an′ ə vʉr′ sər ē) *n.* the date on which something happened in an earlier year [June 14 will be the tenth *anniversary* of their wedding.]
—*pl.* **an′ ni·ver′ sa·ries**

an·nounc·er (ə nouns′ ər) *n.* a person who introduces radio or television programs, reads the news and commercials, etc.

an·nu·al·ly (an′ yoo wəl ē) *adv.* each year; every year.

an·to·nym (an′ tə nim) *n.* a word opposite in meaning to another word ["Sad" is an *antonym* of "happy."]

anx·ious (angk′ shəs) *adj.* **1** having anxiety; worried [Were you *anxious* during the flight?] **2** eagerly wishing [She is *anxious* to do well.] —**anx′ ious·ly** *adv.*

an·y·more (en′ ē môr′) *adv.* now; nowadays [They don't live here *anymore*.]

an·y·where (en′ ē hwer) *adv.* in, at, or to any place [Leave it *anywhere* in my office.]

a·pol·o·gy (ə päl′ ə jē) *n.* a statement that one is sorry [Please accept my *apology* for sending the wrong book.] —*pl.*
a·pol′ o·gies

ap·pear·ance (ə pir′ əns) *n.* **1** the act of appearing. **2** the way a person or thing looks [From his *appearance*, we knew he was angry.]

ap·plaud (ə plôd′) *v.* to show that one enjoys something by clapping one's hands.

ap·point·ment (ə point′ mənt) *n.* an arrangement to meet someone or be somewhere at a certain time [an *appointment* for lunch].

ap·pre·ci·ate (ə prē′ shē āt) *v.* to understand and enjoy [I now *appreciate* modern art.]
—**ap·pre′ ci·at·ed, ap·pre′ ci·at·ing**
—**ap·pre′ ci·a′ tion** *n.*

arch (ärch) *n.* a curved part of a structure that holds up the weight over an open space. Arches are used in doors, windows, bridges, etc. ◆*v.* to form an arch [The bridge *arches* over the river.]

ar·chi·tec·ture (är′ kə tek′ chər) *n.* **1** the planning and putting up of buildings. **2** a style of building [Gothic *architecture* uses pointed arches.] —**ar′ chi·tec′ tur·al** *adj.*
—**ar′ chi·tec′ tur·al·ly** *adv.*

ar·range (ə rānj′) *v.* to put in a certain order [to *arrange* furniture in a room].
—**ar·ranged′, ar·rang′ ing**

ar·range·ment (ə rānj′ mənt) *n.* the way something is arranged [a new *arrangement* of pictures].

ar·riv·al (ə rī′ v'l) *n.* the act of arriving [the *arrival* of spring].

ar·rive (ə rīv′) *v.* to come to a place after a journey [When does the bus from Chicago *arrive* here?] —**ar·rived′, ar·riv′ ing**

a	fat	ir	here	ou	out	zh	leisure
ā	ape	ī	bite, fire	u	up	ng	ring
ä	car, lot	ō	go	ʉr	fur		a *in* ago
e	ten	ô	law, horn	ch	chin		e *in* agent
er	care	oi	oil	sh	she		ə = i *in* unity
ē	even	oo	look	th	thin		o *in* collect
i	hit	oo	tool	th	then		u *in* focus

ar·ti·fi·cial (är′ tə fish′ əl) *adj.* not natural [The flowers are *artificial*.]

ar·ti·fi·cial·ly (är′ tə fish′ ə lē) *adv.* in an unnatural or false way.

-ar·y (er′ ē *or* ər ē) *a suffix meaning:* **1** having to do with [The word *customary* means having to do with customs.] **2** a person or thing connected with [A *missionary* is a person connected with missions.]

as·sem·ble (ə sem′ b'l) *v.* to gather together into a group [The members of the family *assembled* for a reunion.] —**as·sem′ bled, as·sem′ bling**

as·sem·bly (ə sem′ blē) *n.* a group of persons gathered together; meeting. —*pl.* **as·sem′ blies**

as·sign (ə sīn′) *v.* to give out as a task [The teacher *assigned* homework.]

as·signed (ə sīnd′) *adj.* given out [an *assigned* seat].

as·sign·ment (ə sīn′ mənt) *n.* something assigned, as a lesson.

as·sist (ə sist′) *v.* to help [Please *assist* me in preparing the program.]

as·sist·ance (ə sis′ təns) *n.* help; aid.

as·sist·ant (ə sis′ tənt) *n.* a person who assists or helps another [an *assistant* to the president].

as·sort·ed (ə sor′ tid) *adj.* of various kinds; miscellaneous [a box of *assorted* candies].

as·sort·ment (ə sôrt′ mənt) *n.* a collection; variety [an *assortment* of books].

au·thor (ô′ thər) *n.* a person who writes a book or story [The Brontë sisters were the *authors* of novels.]

au·to·bi·og·ra·phy (ôt′ ə bī äg′ rə fē) *n.* the story of one's life written by oneself. —*pl.* **au′ to·bi·og′ ra·phies** —**au′ to·bi′ o·graph′ i·cal** *adj.*

au·to·graph (ôt′ ə graf) *n.* something written in a person's own handwriting, especially that person's name.

au·to·mat·ic (ôt′ ə mat′ ik) *adj.* moving or working by itself [The machinery is *automatic*.] —**au′ to·mat′ i·cal·ly** *adv.*

au·to·mo·bile (ôt′ ə mə bēl′ *or* ot′ ə mə bēl′) *n.* a car moved by an engine.

au·tumn (ôt′ əm) *n.* the season between summer and winter; fall. —**au·tum·nal** (ô tum′ n'l) *adj.*

a·vail·a·ble (ə vā′ lə b'l) *adj.* that can be got, used, or reached [This style is *available* in three colors.] —**a·vail′ a·bil′ i·ty** *n.*

av·er·age (av′ rij *or* av′ ər ij) *adj.* of the usual kind; normal; ordinary [an *average* student].

a·vi·a·tor (ā′ vē āt′ ər) *n.* a person who flies airplanes; pilot.

a·void (ə void′) *v.* **1** to keep away from [to *avoid* crowds]. **2** to keep from happening [Try to *avoid* spilling the milk.] —**a·void′ a·ble** *adj.*

B

bad (bad) *adj.* not good. —**worse, worst** —**bad′ ly** *adv.*

bak·er·y (bāk′ ər ē) *n.* a place where bread, cakes, etc. are baked or sold. —*pl.* **bak′ er·ies**

bank (bangk) *n.* **1** a place of business for keeping, exchanging, or lending money. **2** a place for keeping a supply of something for use later on [The hospital has a blood *bank*.] **3** the land along the side of a river or stream.

bar·o- (bar′ ō) *a combining form meaning* of pressure.

ba·rom·e·ter (bə räm′ ə tər) *n.* an instrument that measures the pressure of air around us. —**bar·o·met·ric** (bar′ ə met′ rik) *adj.*

beau·ti·ful (byo͞ot′ ə fəl) *adj.* very pleasant to look at or hear [She has a *beautiful* face.] —**beau′ ti·ful·ly** *adv.*

beau·ty (byo͞ot′ ē) *n.* **1** that quality in a person or thing that makes it pleasant to look at, hear, or think about [the *beauty* of a sunset]. **2** a beautiful thing or person —*pl.* **beau′ ties**

beige (bāzh) *n., adj.* the color of sand.

belt (belt) *n.* a strip of leather, cloth, etc. worn around the waist.

bi·cy·cle (bī′ si k'l) *n.* a vehicle that has two wheels moved by pedals. —**bi·cy·clist** (bī′ si klist) *n.*

bi·og·ra·phy (bī äg′ rə fē) *n.* the story of a person's life written by another. —*pl.* **bi·og′ ra·phies** —**bi·o·graph·i·cal** (bī′ ə graf′ i k'l) *adj.*

board (bôrd) *n.* **1** a long, flat piece of sawed wood, used in building. **2** a group of people who manage or control a business, etc. ◆*v.* **1** to cover up with boards [The windows were *boarded* up.] **2** to get on a ship, airplane, bus, etc.

bone (bōn) *n.* any of the hard pieces that are joined together to form a skeleton [There are about 200 *bones* in the human body.]

book·shelf (book′ shelf) *n.* a shelf on which books may be kept.

bound·a·ry (boun′ drē *or* boun′ dər ē) *n.* a line or thing that marks the edge or limit [The Delaware River forms the eastern *boundary* of Pennsylvania.] —*pl.* **bound′ a·ries**

brain (brān) *n.* the gray and white tissue inside the skull of a person or of any animal with a backbone.

brave (brāv) *adj.* willing to face danger, pain, or trouble. —**brav′ er, brav′ est** —**brave′ ly** *adv.*

brav·er·y (brā′ vər ē) *n.* the quality of being brave; courage.

break·a·ble (brāk′ ə b'l) *adj.* that can be broken.

broth·er-in-law (bru*th*′ ər in lô′) *n.* **1** the brother of one's husband or wife. **2** the husband of one's sister. —*pl.* **broth′ ers-in-law′**

build·er (bil′ dər) *n.* one that builds; especially, a person whose business is putting up houses and other buildings.

bur·glar (bʉr′ glər) *n.* a person who breaks into a building to steal.

bus (bus) *n.* a large motorcoach for carrying many passengers. —*pl.* **bus′ es**

busi·ness (biz′ nis) *n.* a place where things are made or sold [Pat owns three *businesses*.]

buy (bī) *v.* to get by paying money [The Dutch *bought* Manhattan Island for about $24.] —**bought, buy′ ing** —**buy′ er** *n.*

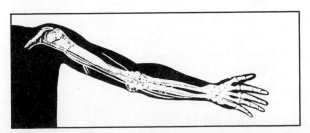

a	fat	ir	here	ou	out	zh	leisure
ā	ape	ī	bite, fire	u	up	ng	ring
ä	car, lot	ō	go	ʉr	fur		a *in* ago
e	ten	ô	law, horn	ch	chin		e *in* agent
er	care	oi	oil	sh	she	ə =	i *in* unity
ē	even	oo	look	th	thin		o *in* collect
i	hit	o͞o	tool	*th*	then		u *in* focus

C

cal·en·dar (kal′ ən dər) *n.* a chart showing an arrangement of time, usually for a single year [an old 1970 *calendar*].

cam·paign (kam pān′) *n.* a series of planned actions [a *campaign* to get someone elected]. —**cam·paign′ er** *n.*

cam·pus (kam′ pəs) *n.* the grounds, and sometimes the buildings as well, of a school or college.

can't (kant) cannot.

ca·reer (kə rir′) *n.* **1** the way one earns one's living [Have you thought of teaching as a *career*?] **2** one's progress through life or in one's work [He has had a long and successful *career* in politics.]

cause (kôz) *n.* a person or thing that brings about some action or result [A spark was the *cause* of the fire.]♦*v.* to make happen; bring about [The icy streets *caused* accidents.] —**caused, caus′ ing**

ceil·ing (sēl′ ing) *n.* the inside top part of a room.

cel·e·ry (sel′ ər ē) *n.* a plant whose stalks are eaten as a vegetable.

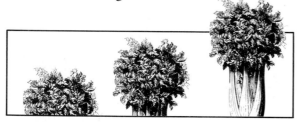

cel·lar (sel′ ər) *n.* a room underground for storing things.

cem·e·ter·y (sem′ ə ter′ ē) *n.* a place for burying the dead; graveyard —*pl.* **cem′ e·ter′ ies**

cen·ter (sen′ tər) *n.* **1** the middle point or part [A vase of flowers is on the *center* of the table.] **2** the main point or place, where there is much activity or attention [a shopping *center*].

chalk (chôk) *n.* **1** a whitish limestone that is soft. **2** a piece of chalk for writing on chalkboards. —**chalk′ y** *adj.*

chem·i·cal (kem′ i k′l) *n.* any substance used in chemistry or got by a chemical process [Various *chemicals* are used in making plastics.] —**chem′ i·cal·ly** *adv.*

chlo·rine (klôr′ ēn) *n.* a greenish-yellow, poisonous gas that is a chemical element.

choir (kwīr) *n.* a group of people trained to sing together.

choose (chōōz) *v.* to pick out one or more from a group [*Choose* a subject from this list.] —**chose, cho′ sen, choos′ ing**

chord (kôrd) *n.* a combination of three or more musical tones that make a harmony when sounded together.

chor·us (kôr′ əs) *n.* **1** a group of people trained to speak or sing together **2** the part of a song that is repeated after each verse; refrain [The *chorus* of "The Battle Hymn of the Republic" begins "Glory, glory, hallelujah!"] —*pl.* **chor′ us·es**

chrome (krōm) *n.* chromium, especially when it is used to plate steel or other metal.

cir·cu·lar ((sʉr′ kyə lər) *adj.* round [a *circular* saw]. —**cir·cu·lar′ i·ty** *n.*

ci·ta·tion (sī tā′ shən) *n.* **1** an order to come to court [A traffic ticket for speeding is a *citation*.] **2** an official mention that praises [to receive a *citation* from the President for bravery].

cite (sīt) *v.* **1** to order to come to court [Jones was *cited* for bad brakes.] —**cit′ ed, cit′ ing 2** to mention for praise [The brave nurse was *cited* in the report.]

cli·max (klī′ maks) *n.* the final idea or event in a series; highest point of interest [The *climax* of the movie came when the children were saved.]

climb (klīm) *v.* to go up by using the feet and often the hands [to *climb* the stairs]. —**climb′ er** *n.*

clothes (klōz *or* klōthz) *n. pl.* cloth or other material made up in different shapes and styles to wear on the body.

col·lar (käl′ ər) *n.* the part of a garment that fits around the neck.

col·or (kul′ ər) *n.* the effect that light rays have on the eyes. ◆*v.* to give color to or change the color of [*Color* the drawings with crayons.]

col·or·ful (kul′ ər fəl) *adj.* full of color [*colorful* wallpaper].

col·umn (käl′ əm) *n.* any articles by one writer or on a special subject, that appear regularly in a newspaper [a chess *column*].

comb (kōm) *n.* a thin strip of plastic with teeth that is passed through the hair to arrange it.

com·bat (kəm bat′ *or* käm′ bat) *v.* to fight or struggle —**com·bat′ ed** or **com·bat′ ted, com·bat′ ing** or **com·bat′ ting** ◆*n.* (käm′ bat) battle [He was wounded in *combat*.]

com·mand (kə mand′) *n.* **1** an order or direction [He obeyed the queen's *commands*.] **2** a military force under someone's control [The general took charge of his new *command*.] ◆*v.* to give an order to [I *command* you to halt!]

com·ment (käm′ ent) *v.* to make remarks [Please *comment* on the book you read.]

com·mer·cial (kə mur′ shəl) *n.* a paid advertisement on radio or TV.

com·mit (kə mit′) *v.* to do something bad or wrong [to *commit* a crime]. —**com·mit′ ted, com·mit′ ting**

com·mit·ment (kə mit′ mənt) *n.* a promise.

com·mit·tee (kə mit′ ē) *n.* a group of people chosen to do a certain thing [a *committee* to plan the party].

com·mon (käm′ ən) *adj.* often seen or heard; usual [Squirrels are *common* in these woods.]

com·mu·ni·ty (kə myōō′ nə tē) *n.* all the people who live in a district, city, etc. [The swimming pool is for the entire *community*.] —*pl.* **com·mu′ ni·ties**

com·pa·ny (kum′ pə nē) *n.* **1** a group joined in work or activity [a business *company*]. **2** a guest or guests [We invited *company* for dinner.] —*pl.* **com′ pa·nies**

com·pare (kəm per′) *v.* to examine certain things in order to find out how they are alike or different. —**com·pared′, com·par′ ing**

com·par·i·son (kəm par′ ə s'n) *n.* a comparing or being compared.

com·plete (kəm plēt′) *v.* to finish or make whole, perfect, etc. [When will the new road be *completed*?] —**com·plet′ ed, com·plet′ ing** —**com·plete′ ly** *adv.*

com·pli·men·ta·ry (käm′ plə men′ tər ē) *adj.* giving praise or admiring.

com·po·si·tion (käm′ pə zish′ ən) *n.* something composed, as a piece of writing or a musical work.

com·press (kəm pres′) *v.* to press into a small space [The air in a tire is *compressed*.] —**com·pres·sion** (kəm presh′ ən) *n.* —**com·pres′ sor** *n.*

com·put·er (kəm pyōōt′ ər) *n.* an electronic device used as a calculator or to store and collect data.

a	fat	ir	here	ou	out	zh	leisure
ā	ape	ī	bite, fire	u	up	ng	ring
ä	car, lot	ō	go	ur	fur		a *in* ago
e	ten	ô	law, horn	ch	chin		e *in* agent
er	care	oi	oil	sh	she	ə = i *in* unity
ē	even	oo	look	th	thin		o *in* collect
i	hit	ōō	tool	th	then		u *in* focus

con- *a prefix meaning* with *or* together; the form of the prefix **com-** that is used before the consonants *c, d, g, j, n, q, s, t,* and *v*.

con·ceit (kən sēt′) *n.* vanity [His *conceit* shows when he talks about how bright he is.] —**con·ceit′ ed** *adj.*

con·ces·sion (kən sesh′ ən) *n.* a right or lease given by a government, company, etc. [the refreshment *concession* at the park].

con·di·tion (kən dish′ ən) *n.* the way a person or thing is [What is the *condition* of the patient?]

con·di·tion·al (kən dish′ ən′l) *adj.* telling of a condition [''If Jane arrives on time'' is a *conditional* clause.] —**con·di′ tion·al·ly** *adv.*

con·duct (kän′ dukt) *n.* the way one acts [The teacher praised the students for their good *conduct*.] ◆*v.* (kən dukt′) to direct; be the leader of [to *conduct* a meeting].

con·duc·tor (kən duk′ tər) *n.* a person who conducts; director [the orchestra *conductor*].

con·form (kən fôrm′) *v.* to be in agreement with [to *conform* to rules]. —**con·form′ a·ble** *adj.* —**con·form′ ist** *n.*

con·nect (kə nekt′) *v.* to join together; unite [Many bridges *connect* Ohio and Kentucky.]

con·sti·tu·tion (kän′ stə too′ shən *or* kän stə tyoo′ shən) *n.* **1** the system of laws of a government, society, etc. **2** a document in which these laws are written [The *Constitution* of the U.S. is the supreme law here.]

con·sti·tu·tion·al (kän′ stə too′ shən'l *or* kän′ stə tyoo′ shən'l) *adj.* of or in agreement with a nation's constitution [Freedom of speech is one of our *constitutional* rights.] —**con′ sti·tu′ tion·al·ly** *adv.*

con·sum·er (kən soo′ mər *or* kən syoo′ mər) *n.* a person who buys goods.

con·tact (kän′ takt) *n.* **1** a touching [The light is turned on by the *contact* of the switch with the wire.] **2** the condition of associating [I come in *contact* with many people.] *v.* to communicate with.

con·tain (kən tān′) *v.* to have in it; hold; enclose or include [This bottle *contains* cream. Your list *contains* 25 names.]

con·tent (kən tent′) *adj.* satisfied [Are you *content* with the food?] ◆*n.* (kän′ tent) the amount held or contained [The *content* of the jar is one liter.] —*pl.* **con·tents** all that is contained.

con·test (kän′ test) *n.* a race, game, etc. in which there is a struggle to be the winner.

con·tin·u·al (kən tin′ yoo wəl) *adj.* happening over and over again [The *continual* banging of the door is annoying.]

con·tin·u·al·ly (kən tin′ yoo ə lē) *adv.* repeatedly [The phone rang *continually*.]

con·tra·dic·tion (kän′ trə dik′ shən) *n.* a contradicting, or saying the opposite of.

con·trar·y (kän′ trer ē) *adj.* opposed [*contrary* to the rules]. ◆*n.* the opposite [Just the *contrary* of what you say is true.]

con·trol (kən trōl′) *v.* to have the power of ruling, guiding, or managing [A thermostat *controls* the heat.] —**con trolled′, con·trol′ ling**

con·ver·sa·tion (kän′ vər sā′ shən) *n.* a talk or a talking together.

con·ver·sa·tion·al (kän′ vər sā′ shən'l) *adj.* of, for, or like conversation. [This author writes in a relaxed, *conversational* style.]

con·vert·i·ble (kən vur′ tə b'l) *adj.* that can be converted ◆*n.* an automobile with a top that can be folded back.

con·vict (kən vikt′) *v.* to judge and find guilty [The jury *convicted* him of robbery.] ◆*n.* (kän′ vikt) a person who is serving a sentence in prison.

con·vince (kən vins′) *v.* to persuade [I'm *convinced* they are telling the truth.] —**con·vinced′, con·vinc′ ing**

cook·er·y (kook′ ər ē) *n.* the art, practice, or work of cooking.

cost (kôst) *v.* **1** to be priced at [It *costs* a dime.] **2** to cause the giving up or loss of [The flood *cost* many lives.] —**cost, cost′ ing** ◆*n.* amount of money, time, work, etc. asked or paid for something [Can you believe the high *cost* of meat?]

couch (kouch) *n.* a piece of furniture for sitting or lying on; sofa.

coun·ter·feit (koun′ tər fit) *adj.* made in imitation of the real thing [The money is *counterfeit.*] ◆*v.* to make an imitation of in order to cheat [He *counterfeited* money.]

crash (krash) *v.* to fall, hit, or break with force and loud noise. ◆*n.* **1** a loud, smashing noise. **2** the crashing of a car, airplane, etc.

crew (kroo) *n.* **1** all the persons working on a ship, aircraft, etc. [This is the ship's *crew.*] **2** any group of people working together [We drove past a road *crew.*]

crime (krīm) *n.* something that is against the law.

crim·i·nal (krim′ ə n'l) *adj.* having to do with crime [*criminal* law]. —**crim′ i·nal·ly** *adv.*

cross-coun·try (krôs′ kun′ trē) *adj., adv.* **1** across open country or fields instead of on roads [a *cross-country* race]. **2** across a country [a *cross-country* flight].

crumb (krum) *n.* a tiny piece broken off, as of bread.

crust (krust) *n.* **1** the hard, crisp, outer part of bread. **2** the shell or cover of a pie, made of flour and shortening. **3** any hard covering or top layer. ◆*v.* to cover or become covered with a crust [The roofs were *crusted* with ice.]

crys·tal (kris′ t'l) *n.* a very clear, sparkling glass.

cue (kyoo) *n.* **1** the last few words in an actor's speech that are a signal to another actor to enter or speak. **2** any signal, hint, or suggestion [If you are not sure which fork to use, take a *cue* from your hostess.] ◆*v.* to give a cue to. —**cued, cu′ ing** or **cue′ ing**

Cue comes from the letter *Q* used in printed play scripts of the 16th and 17th centuries to mark when an actor was supposed to come onto the stage. It is probably an abbreviation for the Latin word *quando,* meaning "when."

cy·clone (sī′ klōn) *n.* a storm with strong winds moving around a center.

Cyclone comes from a Greek word meaning "to circle around" or "to whirl." Cyclones have winds that move around a center in either a clockwise or counterclockwise direction.

cy·press (sī′ prəs) *n.* an evergreen tree with cones and dark leaves.

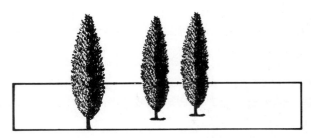

D

dai·ly (dā′ lē) *adj.* **1** done, happening, or published every day or every weekday. **2** calculated by the day [We charge a *daily* rate.] ◆*adv.* every day; day after day.

a	fat	ir	here	ou	out	zh	leisure
ā	ape	ī	bite, fire	u	up	ng	ring
ä	car, lot	ō	go	ur	fur		a *in* ago
e	ten	ô	law, horn	ch	chin		e *in* agent
er	care	oi	oil	sh	she	ə =	i *in* unity
ē	even	oo	look	th	thin		o *in* collect
i	hit	oo	tool	th	then		u *in* focus

dan·ger·ous (dān′ jər əs) *adj.* likely to cause injury, pain, etc.; unsafe [This shaky old bridge is *dangerous*.]
—**dan′ ger·ous·ly** *adv.*

de- (də, dē) *a prefix meaning* away from; down; undo.

debt (det) *n.* something that one owes to another [a *debt* of $25].

de·ceit·ful (di sēt′ fəl) *adj.* lying or misleading. —**de·ceit′ ful·ly** *adv.*
—**de·ceit′ ful·ness** *n.*

de·ceive (di sēv′) *v.* to fool or trick; mislead [The queen *deceived* Snow White by pretending to be her friend.]
—**de·ceived′, de·ceiv′ ing**
—**de·ceiv′ er** *n.*

de·cep·tion (di sep′ shən) *n.* something that fools, as a fraud.

de·cide (di sīd′) *v.* to choose after some thought [I can't *decide* what suit to wear.]
—**de·cid′ ed, de·cid′ ing**

de·code (dē kōd′) *v.* to figure out the meaning of something written in code.
—**de·cod′ ed, de·cod′ ing**

de·duc·tion (di duk′ shən) *n.* **1** subtraction **2** reasoning from facts to a logical conclusion [Detectives solve crimes by *deduction*.]
—**de·duc′ tive** *adj.*

de·flate (di flāt′) *v.* to make smaller or flatter by letting out air or gas [to *deflate* a tire]. —**de·flat′ ed, de·flat′ ing**

de·frost (di frôst′) *v.* **1** to get rid of frost or ice from [to *defrost* a refrigerator]. **2** to become unfrozen.

de·gree (di grē′) *n.* **1** a step in a series [He advanced by *degrees* from office boy to president.] **2** a unit used in measuring temperature that is shown by the symbol °. **3** a unit used in measuring angles and arcs of circles [There are 360 *degrees* in the circumference of a circle.] **4** rank given by a college to a student who has satisfactorily completed a course of study [He got a B.A. *degree*.]

de·hy·drate (dē hī′ drāt) *v.* to remove water from [Powdered milk is milk that has been *dehydrated*.] —**de·hy′ drat·ed, de·hy′ drat·ing** —**de′ hy·dra′ tion** *n.*

de·lay (di lā′) *v.* to put off until a later time; to make late [The bride's illness will *delay* the wedding.] ◆*n.* a delaying [Engine trouble caused a *delay* in the plane's takeoff.]

de·liv·er·y (di liv′ ər ē) *n.* the act of delivering; a distributing [daily *deliveries* to the customers]. —*pl.* **de·liv′ er·ies**

de·pend (di pend′) *v.* to rely for help or support [They *depend* on their parents for money.]

de·pend·a·ble (di pen′ də b'l) *adj.* that can be depended on; reliable [a *dependable* friend]. —**de·pend′ a·bil′ i·ty** *n.*

de·pos·it (di päz′ it) *v.* to place for safekeeping, as money in a bank.

de·press (di pres′) *v.* **1** to make sad or gloomy. **2** to press down [*Depress* the gas pedal.]

de·pres·sion (di presh′ ən) *n.* sadness; gloominess [to suffer from a fit of *depression*].

de·scribe (di skrīb′) *v.* to tell or write about in some detail [to *describe* a trip one has taken]. —**de·scribed′, de·scrib′ ing** —**de·scrib′ a·ble** *adj.*

de·sign (di zīn′) *v.* to arrange the parts of [Who *designed* this book?] ◆*n.* the arrangement of parts, colors, etc.; pattern.

des·ig·nate (dez′ ig nāt) *v.* to point out; show [Cities are *designated* on this map by dots.] —**des′ ig·nat·ed, des′ ig·nat·ing** —**des ig·na′ tion** *n.*

de·sir·a·ble (di zīr′ ə b'l) *adj.* worth wanting or having. —**de·sir′ a·bly** *adv.*

de·stroy (di stroi′) *v.* to put an end to by breaking up, tearing down, or ruining [The flood *destroyed* 300 homes.]

de·tach (di tach′) *v.* **1** to unfasten and take away; disconnect [Five cars were *detached* from the train.] **2** to send on a special task. —**de·tach′ a·ble** *adj.*

de·tect (di tekt′) *v.* to discover something hidden or not easily noticed [I *detect* a slight flaw.]

de·ter·mine (di tʉr′ mən) *v.* **1** to settle or decide on [I haven't *determined* whether to go to college.] **2** resolve [She is *determined* to be a lawyer.] —**de·ter′ mined, de·ter′ min·ing**

di·a- (dī′ ə) *a combining form meaning* through.

di·am·e·ter (dī am′ ət ər) *n.* a straight line passing through the center of a circle.

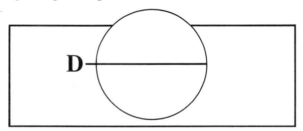

di·a·ry (dī′ ə rē) *n.* a record written day by day of things done, seen, or thought. —*pl.* **di′ a·ries**

dic·ta·tor (dik′ tāt ər) *n.* a ruler who has complete power over a country.

dic·tion·ar·y (dik′ shə ner′ ē) *n.* a book in which words are listed in alphabetical order with their meanings, pronunciations, etc. [a school *dictionary*]. —*pl.* **dic′ tion·ar′ ies**

di·plo·ma (di plō′ mə) *n.* a certificate given to a student by a school or college to show that the student has completed a required course of study.

di·rec·tor (di rek′ tər) *n.* a person who directs the work of others [the *director* of a play, a band, etc.]. —**di·rec′ tor·ship** *n.*

dis- (dis) *a prefix meaning:* **1** away, from, or out of [*Displace* means move away from its place.] **2** the opposite of [*Dishonest* means the opposite of honest.] **3** to fail, stop, or refuse to [*Disagree* means to fail to agree.]

dis·a·gree (dis ə grē′) *v.* to differ in opinion; often, to quarrel or argue [to *disagree* on politics]. —**dis·a·greed′, dis·a·gree′ ing**

dis·ap·pear (dis ə pir′) *v.* vanish [The car *disappeared* around a curb.]

dis·con·nect (dis kə nekt′) *v.* to undo the connection of; separate.

dis·cov·er·y (dis kuv′ ər ē) *n.* a finding out, learning, seeing for the first time. —*pl.* **dis·cov′ er·ies**

dis·pos·al (dis pō′ z'l) *n.* a getting rid of [Take care of the *disposal* of the garbage.]

dis·po·si·tion (dis′ pə zish′ ən) *n.* **1** a getting rid of something [the *disposition* of garbage]. **2** one's nature or mood [a kind *disposition*].

dis·re·spect (dis′ ri spekt′) *n.* lack of respect or politeness; rudeness. —**dis′ re·spect′ ful** *adj.* —**dis′ re·spect′ ful·ly** *adv.*

dis·sat·is·fy (dis sat′ is fī) *v.* to fail to satisfy; leave wanting something more or different. —**dis·sat′ is·fied, dis·sat′ is·fy·ing**

dis·trust (dis trust′) *v.* doubt.

di·vide (də vīd′) *v.* **1** to make separate or keep apart [A stone wall *divides* their farms.] **2** to give out in shares [*Divide* the cake among them.] —**di·vid′ ed, di·vid′ ing**

a	fat	ir	here	ou	out	zh	leisure
ā	ape	ī	bite, fire	u	up	ng	ring
ä	car, lot	ō	go	ʉr	fur		a *in* ago
e	ten	ô	law, horn	ch	chin		e *in* agent
er	care	oi	oil	sh	she	ə = i *in* unity
ē	even	oo	look	th	thin		o *in* collect
i	hit	o͞o	tool	th	then		u *in* focus

doc·tor (däk′ tər) *n.* a person trained to heal the sick.

dol·lar (däl′ ər) *n.* a United States coin or paper money, equal to 100 cents.

doubt (dout) *n.* a condition of being uncertain or not yet decided [The time of the dance is still in *doubt.*] —**doubt′ er** *n.*

dough·nut (dō′ nut) *n.* a small, sweet cake fried in deep fat.

drap·er·y (drā′ pər ē) *n.* a curtain hanging in loose folds. —*pl.* **drap′ er·ies**

drink (dringk) *v.* **1** to swallow a liquid [*Drink* the water.] **2** to soak up or draw in [The dry soil quickly *drank* up the rain.] —**drank, drunk, drink′ ing**

driv·er (drī′ vər) *n.* a person who drives.

du·plex (doo′ pleks) *adj.* having two parts or units [They live in a *duplex* house.] ◆*n.* *a shorter form of* **duplex house.** —*pl.* **du′ plex·es**

dy·nam·ic (dī nam′ ik) *adj.* full of energy or power; forceful [a *dynamic* person]. —**dy·nam′ i·cal·ly** *adv.*

E

ea·gle (ē′ g′l) *n.* a large, strong bird.

earth·quake (ʉrth′ kwāk) *n.* a shaking of the ground.

ech·o (ek′ ō) *n.* a sound heard again when sound waves bounce back from a surface. —*pl.* **ech′ oes** ◆*v.* to be repeated as an echo [Her shout *echoed* in the empty theater.] —**ech′ oed, ech′ o·ing**

e·dict (ē′ dikt) *n.* an order given by a high official, which must be obeyed as law.

ed·it (ed′ it) *v.* to get a piece of writing ready to be published, by correcting or changing the material. —**ed′ i·ted, ed′ i·ting** —**ed·i·tor** (ed′ ə tər) *n.*

ed·i·tor·i·al (ed′ ə tôr′ ē əl) *adj.* of or by an editor [*editorial* offices]. ◆*n.* an article in a newspaper or magazine or a talk on TV or radio that openly gives the opinion of the editor, publisher, or owner.

ei·ther (ē′ thər *or* ī′ thər) *adj.* one or the other of two [Use *either* exit.] ◆*pron.* one or the other [*Either* of the suits will fit you.] ◆*conj.* according to the first of two choices [*Either* come with me or stay home.]

e·ject (i jekt′) *v.* to force out; throw out [The chimney *ejects* smoke.] —**e·jec′ tion** *n.*

el·e·men·ta·ry (el′ ə men′ tər ē) *adj.* having to do with first or simplest things to be learned [*elementary* arithmetic].

e·mis·sion (i mish′ ən) *n.* the act of emitting

e·mit (i mit′) *v.* to send out or give forth [The owl *emitted* a shriek.] —**e·mit′ ted, e·mit′ ting**

em·ploy (im ploi′) *v.* to hire and pay for the work or services of [That company *employs* 50 people.]

en·cy·clo·pe·di·a (in sī′ klə pē′ dē ə) *n.* a set of books that gives information on all branches of knowledge.

The Greek word from which we get **encyclopedia** is made up of three words: *en* meaning "in," *kyklos* meaning "a circle," and *paedea* meaning "education." An encyclopedia is, therefore, a work that deals with all subjects that lie within the circle of education.

en·e·my (en′ ə mē) *n.* a person, group, or country that hates another or fights against another; foe. —*pl.* **en′ e·mies**

en·gi·neer (en′ jə nir′) *n.* **1** a person who is trained to plan and build machinery, roads, bridges, buildings, etc. **2** a person who runs an engine.

en·joy (in joi′) *v.* to get joy or pleasure from [We *enjoyed* the game.] —**en·joyed′, en·joy′ ing** —**en·joy′ ment** *n.*

e·qual (ē′ kwəl) *adj.* of the same amount, size, or value [The horses were of *equal* height.] ♦*v.* to be equal to; match. —**e′ qualed** or **e′ qualled, e′ qual·ing** or **e′ qual·ling** —**e′ qual·ly** *adv.*

e·qua·tor (i kwāt′ ər) *n.* an imaginary circle around the middle of the earth, at an equal distance from North Pole and South Pole.

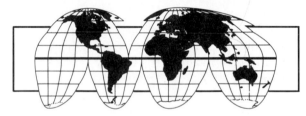

e·quip (i kwip′) *v.* to provide what is needed [The soldiers were *equipped* for battle.] —**e·quipped′, e·quip′ ping**

-er (ər) *a suffix meaning* a person or thing that [A *catcher* is a person that catches.]

er·ror (er′ ər) *n.* **1** a belief, act, etc. that is untrue, incorrect; mistake [an *error* in multiplication]. **2** the condition of being wrong [You are in *error* if you think I don't care.]

-er·y (ər ē) *a suffix meaning:* **1** a place to [A *brewery* is a place to brew.] **2** a place for [A *nunnery* is a place for nuns.] **3** the work of [*Surgery* is the work of a surgeon.] **4** the product of [*Pottery* is the product of a potter.] **5** the condition of [*Slavery* is the condition of a slave.]

ev·er·y·one (ev′ rē wən) *pron.* every person.

ex- (eks) *a prefix meaning* out, from, out of, *or* beyond [To *exhale* is to breathe out. To *exceed* is to go beyond a limit.]

ex·act (ig zakt′) *adj.* not having mistakes; accurate [*exact* measurements]. —**ex·act′ ness** *n.*

ex·act·ly (ig zakt′ lē) *adv.* precisely [That's *exactly* the bike I want.]

ex·ag·ger·ate (ig zaj′ ə rāt) *v.* to make seem greater than it is [He always *exaggerates* when he tells of his adventures.] —**ex·ag′ ger·at·ed, ex·ag′ ger·at·ing** —**ex·ag′ ger·a′ tion** *n.*

ex·am·in·a·tion (ig zam′ ə nā′ shən) *n.* a test.

ex·am·ine (ig zam′ ən) *v.* **1** to look at closely. **2** to ask questions in order to find out how much someone knows [to *examine* a witness in court]. —**ex·am′ ined, ex·am′ in·ing** —**ex·am′ in·er** *n.*

ex·am·ple (ig zam′ p'l) *n.* a model or pattern that is to be copied [Dr. King's life was an *example* of courage to us all.]

ex·ceed (ik sēd′) *v.* to go beyond what is allowed [to *exceed* the speed limit].

ex·cel·lence (ek′ s'l əns) *n.* extra goodness

ex·cel·lent (ek′ s'l ənt) *adj.* very good [The pies are *excellent*!] —**ex′ cel·lent·ly** *adv.*

ex·cept (ik sept′) *prep.* leaving out; other than; but [Everyone *except* you liked the movie.]

ex·cep·tion (ik sep′ shən) *n.* a person or thing that is different from others; case to which rules do not apply [Most mammals do not lay eggs, but the platypus is an *exception*.]

a	fat	ir	here	ou	out	zh	leisure
ā	ape	ī	bite, fire	u	up	ng	ring
ä	car, lot	ō	go	ur	fur		a *in* ago
e	ten	ô	law, horn	ch	chin		e *in* agent
er	care	oi	oil	sh	she	ə = i *in* unity
ē	even	oo	look	th	thin		o *in* collect
i	hit	ōo	tool	th	then		u *in* focus

ex·cep·tion·al (ik sep′ shən′l) *adj.* different or unusual [a class for *exceptional* children]. —**ex·cep′ tion·al·ly** *adv.*

ex·cess (ik ses′ *or* ek′ ses) *n.* too much [Eating an *excess* of candy will harm the teeth.] ◆*adj.* extra [Airlines charge for *excess* luggage.]

ex·cit·able (ik sīt′ ə b′l) *adj.* easily excited. —**ex·cit′ a·bil′ i·ty** *n.*

ex·cite (ik sīt′) *v.* to cause strong feeling in; arouse [The sight of men landing on the moon *excited* the whole world.] —**ex·cit′ ed, ex·cit′ ing**

ex·cite·ment (ik sīt′ mənt) *n.* the condition of being excited [The fire caused great *excitement* in the town.]

ex·claim (iks clām′) *v.* to speak out suddenly and with strong feeling, as in surprise, anger, etc. [''I won't go!'' she *exclaimed*.]

ex·cla·ma·tion (eks′ klə mā′ shən) *n.* a word or phrase that is spoken strongly to show strong feeling, as surprise or anger.

ex·cuse (ik skyōōz′) *v.* **1** to forgive; pardon [Please *excuse* this interruption.] **2** to set free from some duty; release [The busy teacher was *excused* from serving on the jury.] —**ex·cused′, ex·cus′ ing** ◆*n.* (ik skyōōs′) a reason given to explain some action; apology [Ignorance of the law is no *excuse* for wrongdoing.]

ex·e·cute (ek′ si kyōōt) *v.* to carry out [We must *execute* the plan.] —**ex′e·cut·ed, ex′ e·cut·ing**

ex·ert (ig zʉrt′) *v.* to put into use; use [He *exerted* all his strength.]

ex·er·tion (ig zʉr′ shən) *n.* the use of power and strength; effort [The swimmer was worn out by his *exertions*.]

ex·hale (eks hāl′) *v.* to breathe out [Take a deep breath, then *exhale*.] —**ex·haled′, ex·hal′ ing** —**ex·ha·la·tion** (eks′ hə lā′ shən) *n.*

ex·haust (ig zôst′) *v.* **1** to make completely empty [The leak soon *exhausted* the gas tank.] **2** to tire out; weaken [They are *exhausted* from playing tennis.] ◆*n.* the fumes from the engine in an automobile.

ex·haus·tion (ig zôs′ chən) *n.* the condition of being very tired; great weariness.

ex·hib·it (ig zib′ it) *v.* to show or display to the public [to *exhibit* stamp collections]. ◆*n.* something exhibited to the public [an art *exhibit*].

ex·ist (ig zist′) *v.* to live [Fish cannot *exist* long out of water.]

ex·ist·ence (ig zis′ təns) *n.* the condition of being. —**ex·ist′ ent** *adj.*

ex·it (eg′ zit *or* ek′ sit) *n.* **1** a place for going out. **2** departure [We made a quick *exit*.] ◆*v.* to leave.

Exit is a Latin word meaning "he (or she) goes out." It was originally used as a direction to an actor to go off the stage [*Exit* Hamlet.]

---

ex·pel (ik spel′) *v.* to send away as a punishment [Paul was *expelled* from the club because he failed to pay his dues.] —**ex·pelled′, ex·pel′ ling**

ex·plore (ik splôr′) *v.* to travel in a region that is unknown, in order to find out more about it [to *explore* a wild jungle]. —**ex·plored′, ex·plor′ ing** —**ex′ plo·ra′ tion** *n.* —**ex·plor′ er** *n.*

ex·port (ik spôrt′ *or* eks′ pôrt) *v.* to send goods from one country for sale in another [Japan *exports* many radios.] —**ex′ por·ta′ tion** *n.* —**ex·port′ er** *n.*

ex·tend (ik stend′) *v.* to make longer; stretch out [Careful cleaning *extends* the life of a rug.] —**ex·tend′ ed** *adj.*

ex·traor·di·nar·y (ik strôr′ d'n er′ ē) *adj.* very unusual; remarkable [*extraordinary* skill]. —**ex·traor′ di·nar′ i·ly** *adv.*

eye (ī) **n. 1** the part of the body with which a human or animal sees. **2** the iris of the eye [He has blue *eyes*.]◆*v.* to look at [We *eyed* the stranger suspiciously.] —**eyed, ey′ ing**

F

fac·tu·al (fak′ choo wəl) **adj.** containing or based on facts; real; true [a *factual* account]. —**fac′ tu·al·ly adv.**

fa·mil·iar (fə mil′ yər) **adj.** friendly; well-acquainted [a *familiar* face in the crowd].

Familiar comes from the Latin word for "family." Members of a family are very well acquainted. They speak and act in a familiar way with one another.

fa·mil·i·ar·i·ty (fə mil′ yar′ ə tē) **n.** close friendship; intimacy. —*pl.* **fa·mil′ i·ar′ i·ties**

fa·mous (fā′ məs) **adj.** much talked about as being outstanding; very well known.

fare (fer) **v.** to get along [We *fared* well on our trip.] —**fared, far′ ing** ◆*n.* money paid for a trip on a bus, plane, etc. [How much is the *fare* on the subway?]

fash·ion·a·ble (fash′ ən ə b′l) **adj.** following the latest styles; stylish [a *fashionable* hat]. —**fash′ ion·a·bly adv.**

fa·tal (fāt′ ′l) **adj.** causing death [a *fatal* disease]. —**fa′ tal·ly adv.**

fa·vor (fā′ vər) **n.** a helpful and kind action [I did my sick friend the *favor* of shopping for her.]◆*v.* to help [The dark night *favored* his escape.]

fa·vor·a·ble (fā′ vər ə b′l) **adj.** pleasing [She made a *favorable* impression on the critics.] —**fa′ vor·a·bly adv.**

fa·vor·ite (fā′ vər it) **adj.** best liked [Pie is my *favorite* food.]

Feb·ru·ar·y (feb′ rə wer′ ē *or* feb′ yoo wer′ ē) **n.** the second month of the year.

feel (fēl) **v. 1** to touch in order to find out something [*Feel* the baby's bottle to see if the milk is warm.] **2** to be aware of through the senses or the mind [He *felt* rain on his face.] **3** to be or seem to the sense of touch [The water *feels* cold.] —**felt, feel′ ing**

felt (felt) **n.** a heavy material made of wool, fur, or hair pressed together under heat. ◆*adj.* made of felt [She has a *felt* hat.]

fig·ure (fig′ yər) **n. 1** shape, outline, or form [A square is a *figure* with four sides.] **2** a number [the *figure* 8].◆*v.* to find an answer by using arithmetic [*Figure* how much I owe you.] —**fig′ ured, fig′ ur·ing**

fi·nal (fī′ n′l) **adj. 1** coming at the end; last [the *final* chapter in a book]. **2** allowing no further change; deciding [The decision of the judges is *final*.] —**fi′ nal·ly adv.**

flame (flām) **v.** to burn with a flame. —**flamed, flam′ ing**

flash (flash) **v.** to send out a short and bright burst of light [Electric signs *flashed*.] ◆*n.* a short burst of light or something bright [Look at the *flash* of lightning.]

a	fat	ir	here	ou	out	zh	leisure
ā	ape	ī	bite, fire	u	up	ng	ring
ä	car, lot	ō	go	ʉr	fur		a *in* ago
e	ten	ô	law, horn	ch	chin		e *in* agent
er	care	oi	oil	sh	she	ə	= i *in* unity
ē	even	oo	look	th	thin		o *in* collect
i	hit	ōō	tool	*th*	then		u *in* focus

flat·ter·y (flat′ ər ē) *n.* praise that is not really meant. —*pl.* **flat′ ter·ies**

fla·vor (flā′ vər) *n.* the quality of something that is a mixing of its taste and smell [the *flavor* of chocolate].

flight (flīt) *n.* **1** a trip through air, as on an airplane [a 500-mile *flight*]. **2** a fleeing or running away.

fly (flī) *v.* **1** to move through the air by using wings, as a bird. **2** to travel or carry through the air. **3** to move swiftly [Time *flies.*] —**flew, flown, fly′ ing**

folk (fōk) *n.* **1** a people or nation. **2** folk or **folks,** *pl.* people or persons [*Folks* differ in their hobbies.] —*pl.* **folk** or **folks**◆*adj.* of the common people. [This is a *folk* saying.]

for·eign (fôr′ in) *adj.* of, from, or dealing with other countries [*foreign* trade].

for·eign·er (fôr′ in ər) *n.* a person from another country; outsider.

for·feit (fôr′ fit) *v.* to give up something because of what one has done [Because our team was late, we had to *forfeit* the game.]

for·give (fər giv′) *v.* to excuse or pardon [She *forgave* him for his unkindness.] —**for·gave′, for·giv′en, for·giv′ ing** —**for·giv′ a·ble** *adj.*

for·ma·tion (fôr mā′ shən) *n.* the way something is put together; arrangement.

for·ty-two (fôr′ tē·tōo′) *adj.* the number 42

frag·ile (fraj′ ′l) *adj.* delicate [The teacup is *fragile.*]

freight (frāt) *n.* a load of goods shipped by train, truck, ship, etc.

fright·en (frīt′ ′n) *v.* to make afraid; scare [He was *frightened* into confessing.]

fu·el (fyoo′ ′l) *n.* anything that is burned to give heat or power [Coal, gas, oil and wood are *fuels.*]◆*v.* **1** to supply with fuel. **2** to get fuel. —**fu′ eled** or **fu′ elled, fu′ el·ing** or **fu′ el·ling**

fu·ri·ous (fyoor′ ē əs) *adj.* full of fury or wild anger. —**fu′ ri·ous·ly** *adv.*

fur·ther (fur′ thər) *adj., adv.* **1** more; added [I have no *further* news.] **2** more distant.

fu·ry (fyoor′ ē) *n.* wild anger; great rage [She is in a *fury* over her wrecked car.] —*pl.* **fu′ ries**

G

gal·ler·y (gal′ ə rē) *n.* a room, building, or place for showing or selling works of art. —*pl.* **gal′ ler·ies**

gar·den (gär′ d′n) *n.* a piece of ground where flowers, vegetables, etc. are grown. —**gar·den·er** (gärd′ nər) *n.*

gauge (gāj) *n.* **1** a standard for measuring size, thickness, etc. [The *gauge* of a wire tells how thick it is.] **2** any device for measuring something. ◆*v.* **1** to measure exactly the size or amount of. **2** to judge or estimate [How can you *gauge* a person's honesty?] —**gauged, gaug′ ing**

ge·o (jē′ ō) *a combining form meaning* of the earth.

ge·og·ra·phy (jē äg′ rə fē) *n.* the study of the surface of the earth; also the climates, plants, animals, etc. —**ge·og′ ra·pher** *n.*

ge·om·e·try (jē äm′ ə trē) *n.* the branch of mathematics that deals with lines and angles.

ghast·ly (gast′ lē) *adj.* horrible or frightening [a *ghastly* crime]. —**ghast′ li·er, ghast′ li·est** —**ghast′ li·ness** *n.*

ghost (gōst) *n.* a shadowy form that is supposed to be the spirit of a dead person.

gi·ant (jī′ ənt) *n.* **1** an imaginary being that looks like a person but is many times larger and stronger. **2** a person who is especially large, strong, etc.

gi·gan·tic (jī gan′ tik) *adj.* like a giant in size; very big; huge [a *gigantic* building].

glam·or·ous (glam′ ər əs) *adj.* full of glamour; fascinating. —**glam′ or·ous·ly** *adv.*

glimpse (glimps) *v.* to get a quick look at [I *glimpsed* a fox as it ran across the trail.] —**glimpsed, glimps′ ing** ◆*n.* a quick look.

glo·ri·ous (glôr′ ē əs) *adj.* giving, having, or deserving glory or honor [a *glorious* act of bravery].

glos·sa·ry (gläs′ ə rē *or* glôs′ ə rē) *n.* a list of hard words with their meanings. —*pl.* **glos′ sa·ries**

Glossary comes from a Greek word meaning "tongue." Since the tongue is so important in forming words, it is easy to see the connection between the old Greek word and our modern term for a list of words.

gnash (nash) *v.* to grind the teeth together, as in anger or pain.

gnat (nat) *n.* a small insect that bites or stings.

gnaw (nô) *v.* to bite and wear away bit by bit with the teeth [The dog *gnawed* on the bone.]

gnu (nōō *or* nyōō) *n.* a large African antelope.

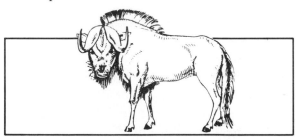

gor·geous (gôr′ jəs) *adj.* magnificent [The tail of a peacock is *gorgeous*.] —**gor′ geous·ly** *adv.*

gov·er·nor (guv′ ər nər) *n.* the person elected head of a state of the United States.

gram·mar (gram′ ər) *n.* **1** a system of rules for speaking and writing a particular language. **2** the way a person speaks or writes, as judged by these rules [His *grammar* is poor.]

grate·ful (grāt′ fəl) *adj.* feeling thankful or showing thanks. —**grate′ ful·ly** *adv.*

great-grand·fa·ther (grāt′ gran′ fä *th*ər) *n.* the male parent of one's grandparent.

gro·cer·y (grō′ sər ē) *n.* **1** a store selling food and household supplies. **2 groceries,** *pl.* the goods sold by a grocer. —*pl.* **gro′ cer·ies**

group (grōōp) *n.* **1** a number of persons or things gathered together. **2** a number of related things that form a class [This is the woodwind *group* of instruments.] ◆*v.* to gather together into a group [*Group* yourselves in a circle.]

guard (gärd) *v.* to watch over; protect; defend. ◆*n.* any person who guards or protects [a museum *guard*].

guess (ges) *v.* to judge or decide about something without having enough facts to know for certain [Can you *guess* how old he is?] ◆*n.* a judgment formed by guessing [Your *guess* is as good as mine.]

guest (gest) *n.* a person who is visiting another's home, or who is being treated to a meal, etc. by another.

gui·tar (gi tär′) *n.* a musical instrument with six strings played by plucking. —**gui·tar′ ist** *n.*

gyp·sy (jip′ sē) *n.* a person who lives a wandering life. —*pl.* **gyp′ sies**

The word **gypsy** comes from an earlier form of Egyptian. It used to be thought that the gypsies had come from Egypt many centuries ago.

a	fat	ir	here	ou	out	zh	leisure
ā	ape	ī	bite, fire	u	up	ng	ring
ä	car, lot	ō	go	ʉr	fur		a *in* ago
e	ten	ô	law, horn	ch	chin		e *in* agent
er	care	oi	oil	sh	she	ə = i *in* unity
ē	even	oo	look	th	thin		o *in* collect
i	hit	ōō	tool	*th*	then		u *in* focus

H

han·dle (han′ d’l) **v. 1** to hold or touch with the hand [*Handle* that china cup with care.] **2** to deal with [There are many ways to *handle* that problem.] —**han′ dled, han′ dling**

hang·ar (hang′ ər) **n.** a shed in which aircraft are kept.

hard·ly (härd′ lē) **adv. 1** only just [I can *hardly* tell them apart.] **2** probably not [That can *hardly* be the best way.]

hatch·back (hach′ bak) **n.** an automobile body with a rear panel that swings up.

haz·ard·ous (haz′ ər dəs) **adj.** dangerous.

height (hīt) **n.** tallness [the *height* of a building].

heir (er) **n.** a person who gets property or a title when the person possessing it dies.

heir·ess (er′ is) **n.** a woman who has inherited or will inherit wealth.

high·land (hī′ lənd) **n.** a region of hills higher than the land around it. —**the Highlands,** the region in northern Scotland. —**high′ land·er** or **High′ land·er n.**

hold (hōld) **v. 1** to take and keep in the hands or arms [*Hold* the baby.] **2** to keep in a certain place or position [*Hold* your head up.] **3** to have room for [This jar *holds* a liter.] —**held, hold′ ing**

hon·or (än′ ər) **n.** glory or credit [the *honor* of winning a Nobel prize]. ♦**v. 1** to show great respect for [America *honors* the memory of Lincoln.] **2** to do something in honor of [We *honored* the team with a banquet.]

hon·or·a·ble (än′ ər ə b’l) **adj.** worthy of being honored. —**hon·or·a·bly adv.**

hor·ri·ble (hôr′ ə b’l) **adj.** causing a feeling of horror; terrible [a *horrible* accident]. —**hor′ ri·bly adv.**

hor·ri·fy (hôr′ ə fī) **v.** to fill with horror [He was *horrified* at the sight of the victims.] —**hor′ ri·fied, hor′ ri·fy·ing**

hor·ror (hôr′ ər) **n.** great fear and disgust [a movie that filled them with *horror*].

hu·mor (hyo͞o′ mər) **n. 1** the quality of being funny [The story is full of *humor*.] **2** the ability to see or express what is funny [She has no sense of *humor*.]

hu·mor·ous (hyo͞o′mər əs) **adj.** funny or amusing; comical. —**hu′ mor·ous·ly adv.**

hy·a·cinth (hī′ə sinth′) **n.** a plant of the lily family with a spike of sweet-smelling flowers.

hy·drant (hī′ drənt) **n.** a closed pipe at a curb with a spout to draw water from a main waterline; fireplug.

hy·phen (hī′ f’n) **n.** the mark (-), used between parts of a compound word (as *court-martial*), or between parts of a word divided at the end of a line.

hyp·no·tism (hip′ nə tiz’m) **n.** the act or science of hypnotizing people.

I

-ic (ik) *a suffix meaning:* **1** of or like [an *angelic* voice]. **2** made or caused by [a *photographic* copy].

i·de·al (ī dē′ əl *or* ī dēl′) **adj.** exactly as one would wish; perfect [Your camp is *ideal* for a vacation.] —**i·de′ al·ly adv.**

i·den·ti·fy (ī den′ tə fī) **v.** to show or prove to be a certain person or thing [She was *identified* by a scar on her chin.] —**i·den′ ti·fied, i·den′ ti·fy·ing**

i·mag·i·nar·y (i maj′ ə ner′ ē) **adj.** that is only in the imagination; not real [Unicorns are *imaginary* beasts.]

im·me·di·ate (i mē′ dē it) *adj.* without delay [The medicine had an *immediate* effect.]
—**im·me′ di·ate·ly** *adv.*

im·mi·grant (im′ ə grənt) *n.* a person who comes into a foreign country to make a new home.

im·mune (i myo͞on′) *adj.* protected against a bad thing, especially a disease, as by a vaccine [*immune* to smallpox].
—**im·mu′ ni·ty** *n.*

im·pend (im pend′) *v.* to be about to happen; threaten [Disaster seemed to be *impending*.]

im·po·lite (im pə līt′) *adj.* not polite; rude.
—**im·po·lite′ ly** *adv.* —**im·po·lite′ ness** *n.*

im·por·tance (im pôr′t′ns) *n.* the fact of being important [news of little *importance*].

im·pos·si·ble (im päs′ ə b′l) *adj.* that cannot be or happen [He found it *impossible* to lift the crate.]
—**im·pos′ si·bil′ i·ty** *n.*
—**im·pos′ si·bly** *adv.*

im·prac·ti·cal (im prak′ ti k′l) *adj.* not useful, efficient, etc.

im·press (im pres′) *v.* to affect the thinking or feelings of [Your quick answers *impressed* us all greatly.]

im·pres·sion (im presh′ ən) *n.* **1** a mark made by pressing [The police took an *impression* of his fingertips.] **2** an effect produced on the mind [The play made a great *impression* on us.]

im·prove (im pro͞ov′) *v.* to make or become better [Business has *improved*.]
—**im·proved′, im·prov′ ing**

im·prove·ment (im pro͞ov′ mənt) *n.* a making or becoming better [Your playing shows *improvement*.]

in- (in) *a prefix meaning:* **1** in, into, within, on, or toward. **2** not [*Incorrect* means not correct.]

in·ca·pa·ble (in kā′ pə b′l) *adj.* not capable; not having the ability or power needed

[*incapable* of helping.]
—**in′ ca·pa·bil′ i·ty** *n.*

in·com·plete (in kəm plēt′) *adj.* without all its parts; not whole or finished.
—**in·com·plete′ ly** *adv.*

in·con·sid·er·ate (in′ kən sid′ ər it) *adj.* not thoughtful of other people.

in·con·ven·ient (in′ kən vēn′ yənt) *adj.* not convenient; causing trouble or bother.

in·de·pend·ent (in′ di pen′ dənt) *adj.* not ruled or controlled by another [Many colonies became *independent* countries after World War II.] —**in′ de·pend′ ent·ly** *adv.*

in·di·vid·u·al (in′ di vij′ oo wəl) *adj.* **1** for or from each single person or thing [*individual* rooms]. **2** personal or unusual.
♦*n.* a single being or person [the rights of the *individual*].

in·di·vid·u·al·ly (in′ di vij′ oo wəl ē) *adv.* one at a time; as individuals [I shall answer each of you *individually*.]

in·duc·tion (in duk′ shən) *n.* being inducted, as into office, a society, or the armed forces.

in·for·ma·tion (in′ fər mā′ shən) *n.* something told or facts learned [An encyclopedia gives *information* about many things.]

in·ject (in jekt′) *v.* to force a fluid into some part of the body [The doctor *injected* the serum in Bob's arm.] —**in·jec′ tion** *n.*

in·jure (in′ jər) *v.* to do harm to; hurt or damage [to *injure* a leg]. —**in′ jured, in′ jur·ing**

a	fat	ir	here	ou	out	zh	leisure
ā	ape	ī	bite, fire	u	up	ng	ring
ä	car, lot	ō	go	ʉr	fur		a *in* ago
e	ten	ô	law, horn	ch	chin		e *in* agent
er	care	oi	oil	sh	she	ə =	i *in* unity
ē	even	oo	look	th	thin		o *in* collect
i	hit	o͞o	tool	th	then		u *in* focus

in·ju·ri·ous (in joor' ē əs) **adj.** harmful or damaging [Smoking can be *injurious* to one's health.]

in·ju·ry (in' jər ē) **n.** harm or damage done to a person or thing [*injuries* received in a fall]. —*pl.* **in' ju·ries**

in·scribe (in skrīb') **v.** to write, print, or engrave [an old tombstone *inscribed* with a verse]. —**in·scribed', in·scrib' ing**

in·scrip·tion (in skrip' shən) **n.** something printed, written, or engraved, as on a coin or a monument.

in·spect (in spekt') **v.** to look at carefully; examine [You should *inspect* the bicycle before you buy it.] —**in·spec' tion n.**

in·tend (in tend') **v.** to have in mind; plan [I *intend* to leave tomorrow.]

Intend comes from a Latin word meaning "to aim at." When we aim or direct the mind toward some purpose, we are intending that it be done.

---

in·ter·jec·tion (in' tər jek' shən) **n.** a word or phrase exclaimed to show strong feeling ["Oh!" and "Good grief!" are *interjections*.]

in·ter·me·di·ate (in' tər mē' dē it) **adj.** coming between two other things or happenings [Adolescence is an *intermediate* stage between being a child and being an adult.]

in·tro·duce (in trə dōōs' *or* in trə dyoos') **v.** to make known; make acquainted [Please *introduce* me to them.] —**in·tro·duced', in·tro·duc' ing**

in·vent (in vent') **v.** be the first to do or make [Who *invented* the telephone?]

in·ven·tor (in ven' tər) **n.** a person who invents.

in·vert (in vurt') **v.** to turn upside down [The image that falls on the film in a camera is *inverted*.]

in·vest (in vest') **v.** to use money for business in order to get a profit. —**in·ves' tor n.**

in·vite (in vīt') **v.** to ask to be one's guest [They *invited* me to dine.] —**in·vit' ed, in·vit' ing**

is·land (ī' lənd) **n.** a piece of land smaller than a continent and surrounded by water.

it's (its) it is.

J

jan·i·tor (jan' i tər) **n.** a person who takes care of a building.

Jan·u·ar·y (jan' yōō wer' ē) **n.** the first month of the year.

jour·ney (jur' nē) **n.** a traveling from one place to another; trip. —*pl.* **jour' neys**

joy·ous (joi' əs) **adj.** full of joy; happy. —**joy' ous·ly adv.**

K

kha·ki (kak' ē) **n.** **1** yellowish brown. **2** a strong, heavy cotton cloth of this color.

kid·ney (kid' nē) **n.** either of a pair of organs in the body that take water and waste products out of the blood. —*pl.* **kid' neys**

knee (nē) **n.** the joint between thigh and lower leg.

knife (nīf) **n.** a tool having a flat, sharp blade, used for cutting. —*pl.* **knives**

knight·hood (nīt' hood) **n.** the rank of a knight.

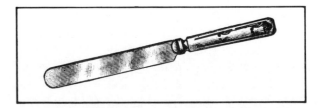

knock (näk) *v.* to rap on a door [Who is *knocking*?]

knuck·le (nuk′ ′l) *n.* a joint of the finger.

L

la·bor (lā′ bər) *n.* work; toil. ◆*v.* to work or toil [Coal miners *labor* underground.]

la·bor·er (lā′ bər ər) *n.* a worker.

lack (lak) *n.* **1** a need for something that is missing [*Lack* of money forced him to return home.] **2** the thing that is needed [Our most serious *lack* was fresh water.] ◆*v.* to be without or not have enough [The soil *lacks* nitrogen.]

laugh·a·ble (laf′ ə b′l) *adj.* causing laughter; funny [a *laughable* costume].

lead·er (lē′ dər) *n.* a person who leads or guides. —**lead′ er·ship** *n.*

leash (lēsh) *n.* a strap or chain by which a dog, etc. is led or held.

le·gal (lē′ gəl) *adj.* allowed by law; lawful [Is it *legal* to park here?] —**le′ gal·ly** *adv.*

lei·sure (lē′ zhər *or* lezh′ ər) *n.* free time not taken up with work. ◆*adj.* not busy [*leisure* time].

lei·sure·ly (lē′ zhər *or* lezh′ ər lē) *adj.* slow [a *leisurely* walk]. ◆*adv.* in a slow, unhurried way [We talked *leisurely*.]

let (let) *v.* **1** permit [They *let* me help.] **2** to allow to pass, come, or go [*Let* them in.] —**let, let′ ting**

li·brar·y (lī′ brer′ ē) *n.* a place where a collection of books is kept for reading or borrowing —*pl.* **li′ brar′ ies**

life·guard (līf′ gärd) *n.* an expert swimmer hired to keep people from drowning.

life·time (līf′ tīm) *n.* the length of time that someone or something lives or lasts.

lik·a·ble (līk′ ə b′l) *adj.* easy to like because pleasing, friendly, etc.

limb (lim) *n.* **1** an arm, leg, or wing. **2** a large branch of a tree.

lis·ten (lis′ ′n) *v.* to pay attention in order to hear [*Listen* to the rain.]

loaf (lōf) *v.* to spend time doing little or nothing [to *loaf* on the job].

loaf·er (lōf′ ər) *n.* a person who loafs.

lo·cal·ly (lō′ k′l ē) *adv.* within a particular place [The storm did much damage *locally*.]

lov·a·ble (luv′ ə b′l) *adj.* that deserves to be loved; easily loved.

lug·gage (lug′ ij) *n.* the suitcases, trunks, etc. of a traveler.

lu·nar (loo′ nər) *adj.* of or like the moon [a *lunar* eclipse; a *lunar* crater.]

lux·u·ri·ous (lug zhoor′ ē əs *or* luk shoor′ ē əs) *adj.* giving a feeling of luxury; rich, comfortable, etc. [a big, soft, *luxurious* chair]. —**lux·u′ ri·ous·ly** *adv.*

lux·u·ry (luk′ shə rē *or* lug′ zhə rē) *n.* the use of the best and most costly thing [a life of *luxury*]. —*pl.* **lux′ u·ries**

-ly (lē) *a suffix used to form adjectives and adverbs, meaning:* **1** of, like, or suitable to [*Friendly* advice is advice like that a friend would give.] **2** every or each [A *weekly* newspaper appears every week.]

lyr·ic (lir′ ik) *adj.* of poetry that describes feelings and thoughts [Sonnets and odes are *lyric* poems.] ◆*n. usually* **lyrics**, *pl.* the words of a song.

M

ma·chine (mə shēn′) *n.* a thing made up of fixed and moving parts, for doing some kind of work [a sewing *machine*].

a	fat	ir	here	ou	out	zh	leisure
ā	ape	ī	bite, fire	u	up	ng	ring
ä	car, lot	ō	go	ʉr	fur		a *in* ago
e	ten	ô	law, horn	ch	chin		e *in* agent
er	care	oi	oil	sh	she	ə =	i *in* unity
ē	even	oo	look	th	thin		o *in* collect
i	hit	oo	tool	th	then		u *in* focus

ma·chin·er·y (mə shēn′ ər ē) *n.* machines in general [the *machinery* of a factory].
—*pl.* **ma·chin′ er·ies**

mag·a·zine (mag ə zēn′ *or* mag′ ə zēn)
n. a publication that comes out regularly and contains articles, stories, pictures, etc.

mag·ic (maj′ ik) *n.* the skill of doing puzzling tricks. ◆*adj.* of or as if by magic.

mag·net (mag′ nit) *n.* any piece of iron, steel, or lodestone that has the natural power to draw iron and steel to it.

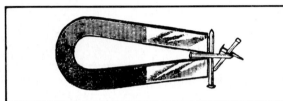

mail·box (māl′ bäks) *n.* a box into which mail is put to be collected for delivery.

ma·jor (mā′ jər) *adj.* greater in size, importance, etc. [the *major* part of his wealth].

make·up (māk′ up) *n.* **1** the way a thing is put together [This is the *makeup* of the atom.] **2** cosmetics. **3** the greasepaint, wigs, costumes, etc. put on by a performer.

man·ag·er (man′ ij ər) *n.* a person who manages a business, baseball team, etc.

man·u·fac·tur·er (man′ yə fak′ chər ər)
n. a person or company that manufactures; especially, a factory owner.

mar·gin (mär′ jən) *n.* the blank space around the writing on a page.

mar·vel·ous (mär′ v′l əs) *adj.* very good; fine; splendid. —**mar′ vel·ous·ly** *adv.*

may·or (mā′ ər *or* mer) *n.* the head of the government of a city or town.

meas·ure (mezh′ ər) *v.* to find out the size of, as by comparing with something else [*Measure* the child's height with a yardstick.] —**meas′ ured, meas′ ur·ing**

meas·ure·ment (mezh′ ər mənt) *n.* size or amount found by measuring.

me·chan·ic (mə kan′ ik) *n.* a worker skilled in using tools or machinery.

med·dle (med′ ′l) *v.* to take part in another's affairs without being asked or wanted [Don't *meddle* in my business.]
—**med′ dled, med′ dling** —**med′ dler** *n.*

me·di·a (mē′ dē ə) *n. a plural of* **medium,** a way of communicating with the general public as TV or newspapers.

me·di·ate (mē′ dē āt′) *v.* to act as a judge in settling a quarrel. —**me′ di·at′ ed, me′ di·at′ ing** —**me′ di·a′ tor** *n.*

me·di·a·tion (mē′ dē ā′ shən) *n.* working to bring about an agreement.

me·di·e·val (mē′ dē ē′ v′l *or* med′ ē ē′ v′l) *adj.* of, like, or belonging to the Middle Ages.

med·ley (med′ lē) *n.* a selection of songs played as a single piece. —*pl.* **med′ leys**

meg·a·phone (meg′ ə fōn) *n.* a large tube shaped like a funnel, through which a person speaks or shouts to send the voice farther.

me·lo·di·ous (mə lō′ dē əs) *adj.* pleasing to hear. —**me·lo′ di·ous·ly** *adv.*

mel·o·dy (mel′ ə dē) *n.* any pleasing series of sounds [a *melody* sung by birds].
—*pl.* **mel′ o·dies**

mem·ber (mem′ bər) *n.* any of the persons who make up a church, club, political party, or other group.

men·tal (men′ t′l) *adj.* of, for, by, or in the mind [He has a good *mental* ability for math.]

men·tal·ly (men′ t′l ē) *adv.* in, with, or by the mind [*mentally* ill; *mentally* alert].

mi·cro·phone (mī′ krə fōn) *n.* a device for picking up sound that is to be made stronger, as in a theater.

mi·cro·scope (mī′ krə skōp) *n.* a device for making tiny things look larger.

mi·cro·scop·ic (mī′ krə skäp′ ik) *adj.* so tiny it cannot be seen without a microscope. —**mi′cro·scop′ i·cal·ly** *adv.*

mil·i·tar·y (mil′ ə ter′ ē) *adj.* of, for, or by soldiers or armed forces [a *military* band]. —**mil·i·tar′ i·ly** *adv.*

mi·nor (mī′ nər) *adj.* lesser in size, importance, etc. [a *minor* part of one's time].

mir·ror (mir′ ər) *n.* a piece of glass coated with silver on the back; looking glass.

mis- (mis) *a prefix meaning* wrong, wrongly, bad, badly [To *misplace* is to place wrongly. *Misconduct* is bad conduct.]

mis·count (mis kount′) *v.* to count incorrectly. —**mis·count′ ed, mis·count′ ing** ◆*n.* (mis′ kount) an incorrect count.

mis·er·y (miz′ ər ē) *n.* a condition in which one suffers greatly or is very unhappy. —*pl.* **mis′ er·ies**

mis·for·tune (mis fôr′ chən) *n.* bad luck; trouble.

mis·judge (mis juj′) *v.* to judge unfairly or wrongly. —**mis·judged′, mis·judg′ ing**

mis·place (mis plās′) *v.* to put in a wrong place [He *misplaced* the book of poems.] —**mis·placed′, mis·plac′ ing**

mis·sion (mish′ ən) *n.* the special duty or errand that a person is sent to do.

mis·sion·ar·y (mish′ ən er′ ē) *n.* a person sent out by a church to spread its religion —*pl.* **mis′ sion·ar′ ies**

mon·arch (män′ ərk) *n.* a ruler, as a king, queen, or emperor.

mon·as·ter·y (män′ ə ster′ ē) *n.* a place where monks live. —*pl.* **mon′ as·ter′ ies**

mo·not·o·nous (mə nät′ 'n əs) *adj.* **1** going on and on in the same tone [He has a *monotonous* voice.] **2** having little or no change [Our trip was *monotonous*.]

most (mōst) *adj.* greatest in amount or degree [Who won the *most* money?]◆*n.* the greatest amount or degree [We spent *most* of our money.] ◆*adv.* **1** in or to the greatest degree or extent [The music pleased me *most*.] **2** very [You have a *most* beautiful dress.]

moun·tain·ous (moun′ t'n əs) *adj.* full of mountains [a *mountainous* region].

mov·a·ble (mo̅o̅′ və b'l) *adj.* that can be moved [*movable* shelves].

mus·cu·lar (mus′ kyoo lər) *adj.* **1** of, made of, or done by muscles [*muscular* effort]. **2** with muscles that are well developed; strong [*muscular* legs]. —**mus′ cu·lar′ i·ty** *n.*

mys·te·ri·ous (mis tir′ ē əs) *adj.* full of or suggesting mystery; hard to explain [*mysterious* crimes]. —**mys·te′ ri·ous·ly** *adv.*

mys·ter·y (mis′ tər ē) *n.* something that is not known or that is kept secret [the *mystery* of life]. —*pl.* **mys′ ter·ies**

Mystery comes from a Greek word that meant "to close the eyes or mouth." A person who was shown secrets of ancient religious ceremonies was not supposed to tell what had been seen or heard.

---

myth (mith) *n.* an old story handed down through the years.

N

na·tion·al (nash′ ə n'l) *adj.* of or having to do with a nation as a whole [a *national* election].

a	fat	ir	here	ou	out	zh	leisure
ā	ape	ī	bite, fire	u	up	ng	ring
ä	car, lot	ō	go	ur	fur		a *in* ago
e	ten	ô	law, horn	ch	chin		e *in* agent
er	care	oi	oil	sh	she	ə =	i *in* unity
ē	even	oo	look	th	thin		o *in* collect
i	hit	o̅o̅	tool	th	then		u *in* focus

na·tion·al·ly (nash′ ə n'l ē) *adv.* throughout the nation, by the whole nation [That television show will be seen *nationally*.]

nat·u·ral (nach′ ər əl) *adj.* produced by nature; not made by man [*natural* resources; *natural* curls]. —**nat′ u·ral·ness** *n.*

nat·u·ral·ly (nach′ ər əl ē) *adv.* in a natural way.

nav·i·ga·tor (nav′ ə gāt′ ər) *n.* a person skilled in figuring the course of a ship or aircraft.

nec·es·sar·i·ly (nes′ ə ser′ ə lē) *adv.* always; inevitably [Cloudy skies do not *necessarily* mean rain.]

nec·es·sar·y (nes′ ə ser′ ē) *adj.* that is needed; required; essential [Do only the *necessary* repairs.]

nei·ther (nē′ thər or nī′ thər) *adj., pron.* not one or the other of two [*Neither* boy went.]

nerv·ous (nur′ vəs) *adj.* restless and easily annoyed or upset [The sound of the guns made the horses *nervous*.] —**nerv′ ous·ly** *adv.* —**nerv′ ous·ness** *n.*

night·time (nīt′ tīm′) *n.* the period of darkness from sunset to sunrise.

nor·mal (nôr′ m'l) *adj.* natural [It is *normal* to make a mistake sometimes.]◆*n.* what is normal [His blood pressure is above *normal*.]

nor·mal·ly (nôr′ mə lē) *adv.* under normal conditions; usually [*Normally* we eat at home.]

nu·cle·ar (noo′ klē ər or nyoo′ klē ər) *adj.* of atomic energy.

numb (num) *adj.* not able to feel [My toes were *numb* with cold.] —**numb′ ly** *adv.* —**numb′ ness** *n.*

nurs·er·y (nur′ sər ē) *n.* **1** a room for the special use of children or infants. **2** a place where young trees or plants are raised. —*pl.* **nurs′ er·ies**

O

ob- (äb, əb) *a prefix meaning* toward, against, before.

oc·cur (ə kur′) *v.* to happen; take place. —**oc·curred′, oc·cur′ ring**

of·ten (ôf′ 'n or ôf′ t'n) *adv.* frequently.

o·mis·sion (ō mish′ ən) *n.* something that is left out.

o·mit (ō mit′) *v.* to leave out [You may *omit* the raisins.] —**o·mit′ ted, o·mit′ ting**

one-way (wun′ wā′) *adj.* that moves or lets one move in one direction only [This is a *one-way* street.]

op·er·a·tor (äp′ ə rāt′ ər) *n.* a person who operates a machine or device [a telephone *operator*].

op·po·nent (ə pō′ nənt) *n.* a person against one in a fight, game, debate, etc.

op·por·tu·ni·ty (äp′ ər too′ nə tē or äp′ er tyoo′ ne tē) *n.* a time that is right for doing something; good chance [You will have an *opportunity* to ask questions after the talk.] *pl.* —**op′ por·tu′ ni·ties**

op·pose (ə pōz′) *v.* to act or be against [The mayor *opposes* raising taxes.] —**op·posed′, op·pos′ ing**

op·po·site (äp′ ə zit) *n.* anything opposite or opposed [Love is the *opposite* of hate.] ◆*prep.* across from; facing [We sat *opposite* each other.]◆*adj.* exactly reverse [Up is *opposite* to down.] —**op′ po·site·ly** *adv.*

op·po·si·tion (äp′ ə zish′ ən) *n.* a fighting against [Our plan met with *opposition*.]

op·to (äp′ tō) *a combining form meaning* of the eye.

op·tom·e·try (äp täm′ ə trē) *n.* the science of examining eyes and fitting with eyeglasses or contact lenses. —**op·to·met·ric** *adj.*

-or (ər or ôr) *a suffix meaning* a person or thing that [An *inventor* is a person who invents.]

or·bit (ôr′ bit) *n.* **1** the path followed by a heavenly body going around another. **2** a single course of a spacecraft or artificial satellite around a heavenly body. ◆*v.* to put or go in an orbit.

or·ches·tra (ôr′ kis trə) *n.* a group of musicians playing together.

or·di·nar·i·ly (ôr′ d'n er′ ə lē) *adv.* usually; generally [I'm *ordinarily* home on Sunday.]

or·di·nar·y (ôr′ d'n er′ ē) *adj.* usual; regular; normal [The *ordinary* price is $10.]

or·gan·ize (ôr′ gə nīz) *v.* **1** to arrange or place according to a system [The library books are *organized* by subject.] **2** to bring into being by working out the details [to *organize* a club]. —**or′ gan·ized, or′ gan·iz·ing** —**or′ gan·iz′ er** *n.*

o·rig·i·nal (ə rij′ ə n'l) *adj.* **1** first or earliest [The *original* settlers of North America were very brave.] **2** new [He had an *original* idea.] **3** being the one of which there are copies [Here is the *original* letter and three copies.]

o·rig·i·nal·ly (ə rij′ ə n'l ē) *adv.* at the start; at first [There were *originally* great herds of bison in America.]

ought (ôt) *a helping verb used with infinitives and meaning* to be forced by what is right, wise, or necessary [He *ought* to pay his debts.]

-ous (əs) *a suffix meaning* having, full of, *or* like [A *courageous* person is full of courage.]

owe (ō) *v.* to be in debt for a certain amount [I still *owe* the bank $200.] —**owed, ow′ ing**

P

paint·er (pānt′ ər) *n.* **1** an artist who paints pictures. **2** a person whose work is painting.

palm (päm) *n.* **1** the inside of the hand between the fingers and wrist. **2** a tree that grows in warm climates.

par·a·lyze (par′ ə līz) *v.* **1** to cause a loss of power or feeling in any part of the body. **2** to make helpless. —**par′ a·lyzed, par′ a·lyz·ing**

par·ent (per′ ənt) *n.* a father or mother.

par·tic·u·lar (pər tik′ yə lər) *adj.* **1** specific [Do you have a *particular* color in mind?] **2** unusual; special [Pay *particular* attention.] —**par·tic′ u·lar·ly** *adv.*

pas·sen·ger (pas′ 'n jər) *n.* a person traveling in a car, bus, plane, etc., but not driving or operating it.

pa·trol (pə trōl′) *v.* to make regular trips around a place in order to guard it. —**pa·trolled′, pa·trol′ ling**

pe·cul·iar (pi kyool′ yər) *adj.* odd; strange [Things look *peculiar* through these dark glasses.] —**pe·cul′ iar·ly** *adv.*

pend·ant (pen′ dənt) *n.* an ornament that hangs down, as a locket or earring.

pen·du·lum (pen′ joo ləm) *n.* a weight hung so that it swings freely back and forth, often used to control a clock's movement.

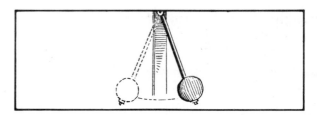

per·ceive (pər sēv′) *v.* **1** to become aware through the senses [to *perceive* the difference between two shades of red]. **2** to take in through the mind. —**per·ceived′, per·ceiv′ ing**

a	fat	ir	here	ou	out	zh	leisure
ā	ape	ī	bite, fire	u	up	ng	ring
ä	car, lot	ō	go	ur	fur		a *in* ago
e	ten	ô	law, horn	ch	chin		e *in* agent
er	care	oi	oil	sh	she	ə = i *in* unity
ē	even	oo	look	th	thin		o *in* collect
i	hit	oo	tool	th	then		u *in* focus

per·cep·tion (pər sep′ shən) *n.* knowledge got by perceiving [She has a clear *perception* of her duty.]

per·form (pər fôrm′) *v.* **1** to do [to *perform* a task]. **2** to do something to entertain an audience. —**per·form′ er** *n.*

per·form·ance (pər fôr′ məns) *n.* **1** a doing [the *performance* of one's duty]. **2** a showing of skill or talent before an audience.

per·i- (per′ ə) *a combining form meaning* around.

pe·rim·e·ter (pə rim′ ə tər) *n.* the boundary or line around an area.

per·ish·a·ble (per′ ish ə b'l) *adj.* that is likely to spoil, as some foods.

per·mis·sion (pər mish′ ən) *n.* consent [You have my *permission* to go.]

per·mit (pər mit′) *v.* to let; allow [Will you *permit* me to help you?] —**per·mit′ ted, per·mit′ ting**

per·pen·dic·u·lar (pur′ pən dik′ yə lər) *adj.* straight up and down; upright [a *perpendicular* flagpole].

per·son·al (pur′ s'n əl) *adj.* of one's own [That is my *personal* opinion.]

per·son·al·ly (pur′ s'n ə lē) *adv.* by oneself, without the help of others [I'll ask them *personally*.]

pho·no·graph (fō′ nə graf) *n.* an instrument for playing records.

pho·to·graph (fōt′ ə graf) *n.* a picture made with a camera.

pho·to·graph·ic (fōt′ ə graf′ ik) *adj.* **1** of or like photography [in *photographic* detail]. **2** used in or made by photography [*photographic* equipment]. —**pho′ to·graph′ i·cal·ly** *adv.*

pil·lar (pil′ ər) *n.* a long, upright structure used as a support for a roof, etc.; column.

plan·et (plan′ it) *n.* any of the large heavenly bodies that revolve around the sun and shine as they reflect the sun's light. The planets, in their order from the sun, are Mercury, Venus, Earth, Mars, Jupiter, Saturn, Uranus, Neptune, and Pluto. —**plan·e·tar·y** (plan′ ə ter′ ē) *adj.*

Planet comes from the Greek word for "wanderer." *Planet* originally meant any of the heavenly bodies that seemed to move or "wander," compared to the stars that seemed to stay always in the same place as seen from the earth.

play·er (plā′ ər) *n.* a person who plays a game or a musical instrument [a baseball *player*; a trumpet *player*].

plumb·er (plum′ ər) *n.* a person whose work is putting in and repairing the pipes in a building.

poi·son·ous (poi′ z'n əs) *adj.* that is a poison; harming or killing by poison [a *poisonous* berry].

po·lar (pō′ lər) *adj.* of or near the North or South Pole.

pop·u·lar (päp′ yə lər) *adj.* **1** having many friends [His quiet humor has made him *popular*.] **2** liked by many people [Pizza is a *popular* food.] —**pop·u·lar·i·ty** (päp′ yə lar′ ə tē) *n.* —**pop′ u·lar·ly** *adv.*

porch (pôrch) *n.* a room on the outside of a building, either open or enclosed by screens, etc.

port (pôrt) *n.* **1** *another word for* **harbor**. **2** a city with a harbor where ships can load and unload.

port·a·ble (pôr tə b'l) *adj.* that can be carried [a *portable* TV].

pose (pōz) *v.* **1** to hold oneself in a certain position for a time. **2** to put in a certain position [The artist *posed* the children.] —**posed, pos′ ing**

po·si·tion (pə zish′ ən) *n.* location [The ship radioed its *position*.]♦*v.* to put in a certain position [They *positioned* themselves around the house.]

pot·ter·y (pät′ ər ē) *n.* pots, dishes, etc. made of clay and hardened by baking.

prac·tice (prak′ tis) *v.* to do something over and over in order to become skilled [She *practices* two hours a day on the piano.] —**prac′ ticed, prac′ tic·ing**

pre- (prē, prə) *a prefix meaning* before [A *prewar* period is a period before a war.]

pre·cise (pri sīs′) *adj.* exact in every detail [The *precise* sum is $12.34.] —**pre·cise′ ly** *adv.*

pre·dict (pri dikt′) *v.* to tell what one thinks will happen in the future [I *predict* that you will win.] —**pre·dict′ a·ble** *adj.*

pre·dic·tion (pri dik′ shən) *n.* 1 the act of predicting. 2 that which is foretold.

pre·fix (prē′ fiks) *n.* a syllable or group of syllables joined to the beginning of a word to change its meaning.

pre·heat (prē hēt′) *v.* to heat ahead of time.

pre·his·tor·ic (prē′ his tôr′ ik) *adj.* of the time before history was written [Dinosaurs were *prehistoric* creatures.] *Also* **pre′ his·tor′ i·cal.** —**pre′ his·tor′ i·cal·ly** *adv.*

prej·u·dice (prej′ ə dis) *n.* 1 an opinion formed without knowing the facts or by ignoring the facts. 2 dislike of people just because they are of another race, religion, etc. ♦*v.* to fill with prejudice. —**prej′ u·diced, prej′ u·dic·ing**

prep·o·si·tion (prep′ ə zish′ ən) *n.* a word that connects a noun or pronoun to something else in the sentence, as to a verb [We went *to* the store], to a noun [the sound *of* music], or to an adjective [good *for* you].

pre·scribe (pri skrīb′) *v.* to order to take a medicine or treatment [The doctor *prescribed* an antibiotic.] —**pre·scribed′, pre·scrib′ ing**

pre·scrip′ tion (pri skrip′ shən) *n.* a doctor's written instructions telling how to prepare and use a medicine; also, a medicine made by following such instructions.

pres·sure (presh′ ər) *n.* a force of pushing or of weight [*pressure* on the brake].

pre·tend (pri tend′) *v.* 1 to make believe [Let's *pretend* we're cowboys.] 2 to act in a false way [She *pretended* to be angry, but she wasn't.]

pre·vent (pri vent′) *v.* to keep from happening [Careful driving *prevents* accidents.] —**pre·vent′ a·ble** *adj.*

pre·view (prē′ vyoo) *v.* to view or show ahead of time.

pride (prīd) *n.* 1 vanity [Her *pride* blinded her to her own faults.] 2 dignity [He has too much *pride* to go begging.] 3 pleasure or satisfaction in something done, owned, etc. [We take *pride* in our garden.]

prob·lem (präb′ ləm) *n.* 1 a condition, person, etc. that is difficult to deal with or hard to understand [Getting the table through the door will be a *problem*.] 2 a question to be solved or worked out [I can do this arithmetic *problem*.]

a	fat	ir	here	ou	out	zh	leisure
ā	ape	ī	bite, fire	u	up	ng	ring
ä	car, lot	ō	go	ʉr	fur		a *in* ago
e	ten	ô	law, horn	ch	chin		e *in* agent
er	care	oi	oil	sh	she	ə = i *in* unity
ē	even	oo	look	th	thin		o *in* collect
i	hit	o͞o	tool	*th*	then		u *in* focus

proc·ess (präs′ es) *n.* a method of making or doing something, in which there are a number of steps [the refining *process* used in making gasoline from crude oil].

pro·duce (prə doos′ *or* prə dyoos′) *v.* **1** to bring forth; yield [trees *producing* apples]. **2** to make or manufacture [a company that *produces* bicycles]. —**pro·duced′ pro·duc′ ing** —**pro·duc′ er** *n.*

pro·fit·a·ble (präf′ it ə b'l) *adj.* that brings profit or benefit [a *profitable* sale]. —**prof′ it·a·bly** *adv.*

proj·ect (präj′ ekt) *n.* a plan, scheme [Our next *project* is to build a raft.] ♦*v.* (prə jekt′) to cause an image to be seen on a surface [to *project* motion pictures on a screen].

pro·pel (prə pel′) *v.* to push or drive forward [Some rockets are *propelled* by liquid fuel.] —**pro·pelled′, pro·pel′ ling**

pro·pel·ler (prə pel′ ər) *n.* a device made up of blades mounted on a shaft, which is turned by an engine for driving an airplane, ship, etc.

prop·a·gan·da (präp′ ə gan′ də) *n.* the spreading of information, ideas, etc. so as to make others accept them.

pros·per (präs′ pər) *v.* to succeed, thrive, etc. in a vigorous way [The town *prospered* when oil was discovered nearby.]

pros·per·ous (präs′ pər əs) *adj.* successful, well-off, thriving, etc. [a *prosperous* business.] —**pros′ per·ous·ly** *adv.*

pro·te·in (prō′ tēn) *n.* a substance containing nitrogen and other elements, found in all living things and in such foods as cheese, meat, eggs, etc.

pub·lish (pub′ lish) *v.* to prepare and bring out a book, magazine, newspaper, etc. as for sale.

pub·lish·er (pub′ lish ər) *n.* a person that publishes books, magazines, newspapers, etc.

punc·tu·al (pungk′ choo wəl) *adj.* coming, or doing something, at the right time; prompt. —**punc′ tu·al′ i·ty** *n.* —**punc′ tu·al·ly** *adv.*

pun·ish·a·ble (pun′ ish ə b'l) *adj.* that can or should be punished [a *punishable* crime].

pur·chase (pur′ chis) *v.* to buy [to *purchase* a car]. —**pur′ chased, pur′ chas·ing** —**pur′ chas·er** *n.*

pur·pose (pur′ pəs) *n.* **1** what one plans to get or do [I came for the *purpose* of speaking to you.] **2** the reason or use for something [This room serves no *purpose*.]

put (poot) *v.* **1** place; set [*Put* soap in the water.] **2** to give or assign [The government *put* a tax on luxuries.] —**put, put′ ting** —**put on** to present, as a play on stage.

pyr′ a·mid (pir′ ə mid) *n.* **1** a solid figure whose sides are triangles that come together in a point at the top. **2** any of the huge structures in which ancient Egyptian rulers were buried.

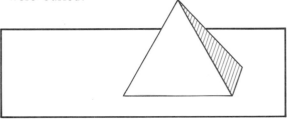

py·thon (pī′ thän *or* pī′ thən) *n.* a very large snake that twists around its prey and crushes it to death.

R

rack (rak) *n.* **1** a framework, stand, etc. for holding things [Put your clothes on the clothes *rack*.] **2** a device for lifting an automobile so that it can be repaired from below.

raise (rāz) *v.* to cause to rise; lift [*Raise* your hand if you have a question.] —**raised, rais′ ing**

ramp (ramp) *n.* **1** a sloping road, walk, surface, etc. going from a lower to a higher place. **2** a staircase on wheels rolled up to a plane for people to use in getting on or off.

rash (rash) *n.* a breaking out of red spots on the skin [The measles gave her a *rash*.]

rasp·ber·ry (raz′ ber′ ē) *n.* a small red or black fruit with many seeds. —*pl.* **rasp′ ber′ ries**

re- (rē, ri, rə) *a prefix meaning*: **1** again [To *reappear* is to appear again.] **2** back [To *repay* is to pay back.]

reach (rēch) *v.* to go as far as; get to [The climbers *reached* the top of Mt. Everest.]

reach·a·ble (rēch′ ə b'l) *adj.* that which can be reached.

read·a·ble (rēd′ ə b'l) *adj.* that can be read; legible [My handwriting is quite *readable*.]

re·al (rē′ əl *or* rēl) *adj.* **1** not imagined [He could hardly believe that his luck was *real*.] **2** genuine [Are these *real* pearls?]

re·al·ly (rē′ ə lē *or* rēl′ ē) *adv.* in fact; truly [I am not *really* angry.]

re·ar·range (rē ə rānj′) *v.* to arrange again or in a different way. —**re·ar·ranged′, re·ar·rang′ ing** —**re·ar·range′ ment** *n.*

rea·son·a·ble (rē′ zən ə b'l) *adj.* **1** sensible. **2** not too high or too low; fair [a *reasonable* price]. —**rea′ son·a·bly** *adv.*

re·call (re kôl′) *v.* **1** to bring back to mind; remember [Can you *recall* how you felt?] **2** to call back; order to return [The ambassador was *recalled* to Washington.]

re·ceipt (ri sēt′) *n.* a written statement that something has been received [My landlord gave me a *receipt* when I paid my rent.]

re·cep·ta·cle (ri sep′ tə k'l) *n.* anything used to keep something in [a trash *receptacle*].

re·cep·tive (ri sep′ tiv) *adj.* able or ready to receive ideas, requests, etc. [The teacher was *receptive* to his student's idea.]

re·cess (rē′ ses) *n.* a stopping of work for a short time, to relax. ◆*v.* (ri ses′) to stop work, study, etc. for a while.

re·cit·al (ri sīt′ 'l) *n.* a program of music or dances.

re·cite (ri sīt′) *v.* to say aloud before an audience [to *recite* the Gettysburg Address]. —**re·cit′ ed, re·cit′ ing** —**re·cit′ er** *n.*

rec·og·nize (rek′ əg nīz) *v.* to be aware of as something seen, heard, etc. before [to *recognize* a street]. —**rec′ og·nized, rec′ og·niz·ing**

re·con·sid·er (rē kən sid′ ər) *v.* to think about again.

rec·tan·gu·lar (rek tang′ gyə lər) *adj.* shaped like a rectangle [a *rectangular* field].

re·duce (ri d̅o̅o̅s′ *or* ri dy̅o̅o̅s′) *v.* to make smaller, less, fewer, etc. [to *reduce* speed; to *reduce* taxes]. —**re·duced′, re·duc′ ing** —**re·duc′ er** *n.* —**re·duc′ i·ble** *adj.*

re·en·ter (rē en′ tər) *v.* to come back in again. —**re·en′ try** *n.*

re·fin·er·y (ri fīn′ ər ē) *n.* a place where raw material, such as oil or sugar, is refined or purified. —*pl.* **re·fin′ er·ies**

re·flect (ri flekt′) *v.* **1** to throw back, as light, heat, or sound [A polished metal surface *reflects* light.] **2** to give back an image of [The calm lake *reflected* the trees.]

re·form (ri fôrm′) *v.* to improve [We must *reform* the working conditions in this factory.]

a	fat	ir	here	ou	out	zh	leisure
ā	ape	ī	bite, fire	u	up	ng	ring
ä	car, lot	ō	go	ur	fur		a *in* ago
e	ten	ô	law, horn	ch	chin		e *in* agent
er	care	oi	oil	sh	she	ə =	i *in* unity
ē	even	oo	look	th	thin		o *in* collect
i	hit	o̅o̅	tool	th	then		u *in* focus

re·fresh (ri fresh′) *v.* to make fresh again [A soft rain *refreshed* the wilted plants.]

re·frig·er·a·tor (ri frig′ ə rāt′ ər) *n.* a box in which the air is kept cool to keep food from spoiling.

re·fund (ri fund′) *v.* to give back money, etc. [We will *refund* the full price.] ♦*n.* (rē′ fund) the act of refunding or the amount refunded. —**re·fund′ a·ble** *adj.*

reg·i·ment (rej′ ə mənt) *n.* a unit of soldiers, made up of two or more battalions [an army *regiment*]. —**reg′ i·men′ tal** *adj.* —**reg′ i·men·ta′ tion** *n.*

reg·is·ter (rej′ is tər) *n.* a record or list of names, events, or things [a hotel *register*]. ♦*v.* to keep a record of in a register [to *register* a birth].

re·gret (ri gret′) *v.* to be sorry for something that has happened [to *regret* the loss of a pet]. —**re·gret′ ted, re·gret′ ting**

reg·u·lar (reg′ yə lər) *adj.* usual; customary [Sit in your *regular* place.] —**reg·u·lar·i·ty** (reg′ yə lar′ ə tē) *n.* —**reg′ u·lar·ly** *adv.*

reg·u·late (reg′ yə lāt) *v.* to fix at a certain speed, amount, etc.; adjust to some standard [*regulate* the heat]. —**reg′ u·lat·ed, reg′ u·lat·ing** —**reg′ u·la′ tor** *n.*

reign (rān) *v.* to rule as a king, queen, etc. [Henry VIII *reigned* for 38 years.]

re·in·vest (rē′ in vest′) *v.* to invest again.

re·ject (ri jekt′) *v.* **1** to refuse to take, accept, use, etc. [to *reject* advice]. **2** to throw away as worthless [The school *rejected* the old books.] ♦*n.* (rē′ jekt) something thrown away. —**re·jec′ tion** *n.*

re·lax (ri laks′) *v.* **1** loosen up [The body *relaxes* in sleep.] **2** to rest from work or effort [He *relaxes* by going fishing.]

re·ly (ri lī′) *v.* to trust or depend [You can *rely* on me.] —**re·lied′, re·ly′ ing**

re·main·der (ri mān′ dər) *n.* the part, number, etc. left over [I sold some books and gave the *remainder* to the library.]

re·mit·tance (ri mit′ ′ns) *n.* money sent in payment.

re·mod·el (rē mäd′ ′l) *v.* to make over; rebuild [to *remodel* a kitchen]. —**re·mod′ eled, re·mod′ el·ing**

re·move (ri mōōv′) *v.* to get rid of [to *remove* a stain]. —**re·moved′, re·mov′ ing** —**re·mov′ a·ble** *adj.* —**re·mov′ er** *n.*

re·new (ri nōō′ *or* ri nyōō′) *v.* to make new or fresh again [*Renew* that old table by painting it.] —**re·new′ al** *n.*

re·peat (ri pēt′) *v.* to say again [Will you *repeat* that question?]

re·port·er (ri pôrt′ ər) *n.* a person who gathers and writes about news for newspapers, radio, or TV.

re·quire (ri kwīr′) *v.* to be in need of [Most plants *require* sunlight.] —**re·quired′, re·quir′ ing**

re·quire·ment (ri kwīr′ mənt) *n.* something needed or demanded [Vitamins are a *requirement* in the diet.]

re·sign (ri zīn′) *v.* to give up one's office, position, membership, etc. [The governor had to *resign* when she became ill.]

res·ig·na·tion (rez′ ig nā′ shən) *n.* the act of resigning.

re·spect (ri spekt′) *v.* **1** to feel or show honor for [We *respect* learned people.] **2** to be thoughtful about [to *respect* others' rights]. ♦*n.* a feeling of honor or polite regard [He has great *respect* for his father.]

re·spect·a·ble (ri spek′ tə b′l) *adj.* having a good reputation. —**re·spect′ a·bil′ i·ty** *n.* —**re·spect′ a·bly** *adv.*

re·spond (ri spänd′) *v.* to answer; reply [You didn't *respond* to my question.]

re·sult (ri zult′) *v.* to happen because of something else [Floods may *result* from heavy rains.] ♦*n.* effect; outcome [The juggler's skill is the *result* of practice.]

re·sume (ri zōōm′) **v.** to begin again [The game will be *resumed* when the rain stops.] —**re·sumed′, re·sum′ ing**

re·tire (ri tīr′) **v.** to give up one's work because of age [Dr. Miller is 84, but refuses to *retire*.] —**re·tired′, re·tir′ ing** —**re·tire′ ment n.**

re·verse (ri vʉrs′) **adj.** causing a car, etc. to move backward [a *reverse* gear]. ◆**n.** a reverse gear [Shift into *reverse* and back up.] ◆**v.** to go or make go in an opposite direction. —**re·versed′, re·vers′ ing**

re·view (ri vyōō′) **v.** to go over or study again [*Review* the information for your test.]

re·vise (ri vīz′) **v.** **1** make different [to *revise* one's opinion]. **2** to read carefully and change in order to make better [to *revise* a history book]. —**re·vised′, re·vis′ ing**

rev·o·lu·tion·ar·y (rev′ ə lōō′ shən er′ ē) **adj.** bringing about great change [a *revolutionary* new way to make glass]. ◆**n.** a person who is in favor of or causing a revolution. —*pl.* **rev′o·lu′tion·ar′ies**

re·ward (ri wôrd′) **n.** **1** something given in return [He got a *reward* for bravery.] **2** money offered, as for returning something lost. —*pl.* **re·wards′** ◆**v.** to give a reward to or for.

rhine·stone (rīn′ stōn) **n.** an artificial gem made of glass, cut to look like a diamond.

rhi·noc·er·os (rī näs′ ər əs) **n.** a large animal with a thick skin, found in Africa and Asia.

rho·do·den·dron (rō′ də den′ drən) **n.** a shrub that bears flowers of pink, white, or purple.

rhu·barb (rōō′ bärb) **n.** a plant with large leaves and thick sour stalks used as food.

rhum·ba (rum′ bə) **n.** a dance of Cuban origin with a complex rhythm.

rhyme (rīm) **n.** **1** a word that has the same end sound as another ["Single" is a *rhyme* for "tingle."] **2** poetry using such end sounds.

rhythm (ri*th*′ 'm) **n.** a movement in which the sounds follow a pattern, with beats at certain times [the *rhythm* of the heart, of the waves, of dancing].

rich (rich) **adj.** **1** having wealth. **2** having much of something [Tomatoes are *rich* in vitamin C.] **3** worth much [You got a *rich* prize.] —**rich′ ly adv.**

ri·dic·u·lous (ri dik′ yə ləs) **adj.** foolish; absurd. —**ri·dic′ u·lous·ly adv.**

risk (risk) **n.** the chance of getting hurt, or of losing, failing, etc. [He ran into the burning house at the *risk* of his life.] ◆**v.** **1** put in danger [You are *risking* your health by smoking.] **2** to take the chance of [Are you willing to *risk* a fight for your beliefs?]

rob·ber·y (räb′ ər ē) **n.** the act of robbing; theft. —*pl.* **rob′ ber·ies**

role (rōl) **n.** **1** the part that an actor takes in a play [She has the heroine's *role*.] **2** a part that a person plays in life [He does a good job in his *role* as a scoutmaster.]

room·mate (rōōm′ māt) **n.** a person with whom one shares a room or rooms.

a	fat	ir	here	ou	out	zh	leisure
ā	ape	ī	bite, fire	u	up	ng	ring
ä	car, lot	ō	go	ʉr	fur		a *in* ago
e	ten	ô	law, horn	ch	chin		e *in* agent
er	care	oi	oil	sh	she	ə =	i *in* unity
ē	even	oo	look	th	thin		o *in* collect
i	hit	ōō	tool	*th*	then		u *in* focus

rou·tine (rōō tēn′) *n.* **1** a regular way of doing something [I have a daily *routine* I follow.] **2** a series of steps for a dance. ◆*adj.* of, using, or done by routine [This is a *routine* task.]

ru·mor (rōō′ mər) *n.* a story told as news, which may or may not be true and which is passed on from person to person [I heard a *rumor* that they were married.] ◆*v.* to tell as a rumor [It has been *rumored* that Pat is leaving school.]

S

sal·a·ry (sal′ ə rē) *n.* a fixed amount of money paid at regular times for work done. —*pl.* **sal′ a·ries**

Salary comes from a Latin word that means money for salt, as part of a Roman soldier's pay. To be worth one's salt is to be worth one's salary or wage.

salm·on (sam′ ən) *n.* a large food fish that is orange pink when cooked. —*pl.* **salm′ on** or **salm′ ons**

sand·wich (sand′ wich) *n.* slices of bread with a filling between them.

The **sandwich** was named after the 4th Earl of Sandwich (1718–1792). He ate his bread and meat this way so that he would not have to leave the gambling table to eat a regular meal.

san·i·tar·y (san′ ə ter′ ē) *adj.* free from dirt; clean [a *sanitary* meat market].

sat·is·fy (sat′ is fī) *v.* to meet the needs or wishes of; please [Only first prize will *satisfy* him.] —**sat′ is·fied, sat′ is·fy·ing**

sce·ner·y (sē′ nər ē) *n.* **1** outdoor views [the *scenery* along the shore]. **2** painted screens, etc. used on stage for a play.

sched·ule (skej′ ool) *n.* a list of the times at which certain things are to happen; timetable [a *schedule* of the sailings of an ocean liner].

scho·las·tic (skə las′ tik) *adj.* having to do with schools, students, teachers, and studies [He was awarded *scholastic* honors.] —**scho·las′ ti·cal·ly** *adv.*

school (skōōl) *n.* a place for teaching and learning, as a public school, college, etc. ◆*adj.* of or for a school [our *school* band].

School comes from a Greek word that means "leisure or free time" and also "what one does in one's free time." Most young people have the free time to go to school because they do not work.

scrib·ble (skrib′ 'l) *v.* to write quickly or carelessly. —**scrib′ bled, scrib′ bling** ◆*n.* scribbled writing. —**scrib′ bler** *n.*

scribe (skrīb) *n.* a person who wrote out copies of books before the invention of printing.

search (surch) *v.* to look through to find something [We *searched* the house.] ◆*n.* the act of searching.

sec·re·tar·y (sek′ rə ter′ ē) *n.* a person whose work is writing letters, etc. for a person, organization, etc. —*pl.* **sec′ re·tar′ ies** —**sec·re·tar·i·al** (sek′ re ter′ ē əl) *adj.*

seem (sēm) *v.* **1** to have the look of being; appear to be [You *seem* happy.] **2** to appear to be true [It *seems* I was right.]

seize (sēz) *v.* **1** to take hold of in a sudden way [to *seize* a weapon]. **2** to capture or arrest. **3** to take over by force [The troops *seized* the fort.] —**seized, seiz′ ing**

self- (self) *a prefix meaning*: **1** to oneself [A *self*-addressed envelope is addressed to oneself.] **2** for oneself [*Self*-pity is pity for oneself.]

self-addressed (self ə drest′) *adj.* addressed to oneself.

sen·a·tor (sen′ ə tər) *n.* a member of a senate. —**sen·a·to·ri·al** (sen′ ə tôr′ ē əl) *adj.*

sep·a·rate (sep′ ə rāt) *v.* divide into parts or groups [*Separate* the good apples from the bad ones.] —**sep′ a·rat·ed, sep′ a·rat·ing** ♦*adj.* (sep′ ər it *or* sep′ rit) not joined; single.

set·ting (set′ ing) *n.* **1** the act of one that sets. **2** the thing in which something is set [The ruby was in a gold *setting*.] **3** the time, place, and circumstances of an event, story, play, etc.

she's (shēz) **1** she is. **2** she has.

shoot (sho͞ot) *v.* to send out with force from a gun, bow, etc. [*Shoot* the bullets.] —**shot, shoot′ ing**

shot (shät) *n.* **1** the act or sound of shooting a gun or cannon [I heard a *shot*.] **2** an attempt to hit something [The first *shot* missed.] **3** an injection.

shut·tle (shut′ 'l) *n.* a bus, train, or airplane that makes frequent trips back and forth over a short route. —*pl.* **shut′ tles** ♦*v.* to move rapidly to and fro. —**shut′ tled, shut′ tling**

sigh (sī) *v.* to let out a long breath, usually to show that one is sad, tired, etc.

sight·se·er (sīt′ sē′ ər) *n.* a person who goes about to see places and things of interest.

sight·see·ing (sīt′ sē′ ing) *n.* going about to see places of interest.

sign (sīn) *n.* a board put up in public with information [The *sign* said, "Do not enter."] ♦*v.* to write one's name on.

sig·na·ture (sig′ nə chər) *n.* a person's name as he or she has written it.

si·lent (sī′ lənt) *adj.* **1** not speaking much. **2** noiseless [Find a *silent* place to study.] **3** not spoken or told [There is a *silent* "b" in "debt."] —**si′ lent·ly** *adv.*

sil·ver (sil′ vər) *n.* **1** a white precious metal that is a chemical element. **2** silver coins or tableware. **3** the grayish-white color of silver. ♦*adj.* **1** of or containing silver [Get the *silver* tray.] **2** having the color of silver.

sim·i·lar (sim′ ə lər) *adj.* almost but not exactly the same [Your ideas are *similar* to mine.] —**sim′ i·lar·ly** *adv.*

sim·i·lar·i·ty (sim′ ə lar′ ə tē) *n.* a similar point or feature. —*pl.* **sim′ i·lar′ i·ties**

sin·gu·lar (sing′ gyə lər) *adj.* showing that only one is meant [The *singular* form of "geese" is "goose."] —**sin′ gu·lar·ly** *adv.* —**sin′ gu·lar′ i·ty** *n.*

si·nus (sī′ nəs) *n.* any of the cavities in the bones of the skull that open into the nose.

sit (sit) *v.* **1** to rest the weight of the body upon the buttocks or haunches [She is *sitting* on a bench.] **2** to perch, rest, lie, etc. [A bird *sat* on the fence.] —**sat, sit′ ting**

skill (skil) *n.* **1** ability that comes from training, practice, etc. [He plays the violin with *skill*.] **2** an art, craft, or science [Weaving is a *skill* often taught to the blind.]

slav·er·y (slā′ və rē) *n.* **1** the practice of owning slaves [The 13th Amendment abolished *slavery* in the U.S.] **2** the condition of being a slave; bondage [Joseph was sold into *slavery*.]

a	fat	ir	here	ou	out	zh	leisure
ā	ape	ī	bite, fire	u	up	ng	ring
ä	car, lot	ō	go	ʉr	fur		a *in* ago
e	ten	ô	law, horn	ch	chin		e *in* agent
er	care	oi	oil	sh	she	ə =	i *in* unity
ē	even	oo	look	th	thin		o *in* collect
i	hit	o͞o	tool	th	then		u *in* focus

sleigh (slā) *n.* a carriage with runners for travel over snow or ice. ♦*v.* to ride in or drive a sleigh.

slip·per·y (slip′ ər ē) *adj.* that can cause slipping [Wet streets are *slippery*.]
—**slip′ per·i·er, slip′ per·i·est**

slo·gan (slō′ gən) *n.* a word or phrase used to get attention or to advertise.

smooth (smo͞oth) *adj.* **1** having an even surface [There is *smooth* water on the lake.] **2** even or gentle in movement [We had a *smooth* airplane flight.]♦*v.* to make smooth or even [*Smooth* the board with sandpaper.]
—**smooth′ ly** *adv.*

soar (sôr) *v.* **1** to rise or fly high in the air [The plane *soared* out of sight.] **2** to rise above what is usual [Prices *soared* after the war.]

so·da (sō′ də) *n.* **1** any of certain substances containing sodium. **2** *a shorter name for* **soda water**. **3** a drink made of soda water, syrup, and ice cream.

so·lar (sō′ lər) *adj.* of or having to do with the sun [a *solar* eclipse; *solar* energy].

sol·emn (säl′ əm) *adj.* serious; very earnest [a *solemn* oath]. —**sol′ emn·ly** *adv.*

sol·id (säl′ id) *adj.* keeping its shape instead of flowing or spreading out [Ice is water in a *solid* form.] **2** not hollow [a *solid* block of wood]. **3** that has length, width, and thickness [A prism is a *solid* figure.] **4** strong, firm, sound, dependable [a *solid* building]. ♦*n.* something that is solid [Iron and glass are *solids*.] —**sol′ id·ly** *adv.*

solve (sälv) *v.* to find the answer to; make clear [to *solve* a problem in arithmetic].
—**solved, solv′ ing**

space·craft (spās′ kraft) *n.* any spaceship or satellite designed for use in outer space.
—*pl.* **space′ craft**

spa·ghet·ti (spə get′ ē) *n.* long strings of flour paste, cooked and served with a sauce.

Spaghetti comes from the plural of the Italian word for "little cord." Spaghetti looks very much like little cords, or strings, especially after it is cooked.

speak·er (spē′ kər) *n.* a person who speaks or makes speeches.

spec·ta·cle (spek′ tə k'l) *n.* an unusual sight or a grand public show [The fireworks display was a *spectacle*.]

Spectacle comes from the Latin word meaning "to behold." A spectacle is something to look at.

spec·tac·u·lar (spek tak′ yə lər) *adj.* showy; striking [a *spectacular* display of roses].
—**spec·tac′ u·lar·ly** *adv.*

spec·ta·tor (spek′ tāt′ ər) *n.* a person who watches without taking part; onlooker [We were *spectators* at the World Series.]

speech (spēch) *n.* a talk given in public [political *speeches* on TV].

spon·sor (spän′ sər) *n.* a person who agrees to be responsible for another person or thing, as in paying expenses.

stair (ster) *n.* **1** one of a series of steps going up or down. **2** *usually* **stairs**, *pl.* a flight of steps; staircase.

starve (stärv) *v.* to die or suffer from lack of food. —**starved, starv' ing**

state (stāt) *v.* to tell in a formal way [The coach *stated* the rules.] —**stat'ed, stat' ing**

state·ment (stāt' mənt) *n.* something stated or said [May we quote your *statement*?]

sta·tion·ar·y (stā' shə ner' ē) *adj.* not to be moved [*stationary* seats].

sta·tion·er·y (stā' shə ner' ē) *n.* paper, envelopes, etc. for writing letters.

steer (stir) *v.* **1** to guide or direct the movement of [She *steered* the car into the garage.] **2** to be steered [This car *steers* easily.]

stom·ach (stum' ək) *n.* the large, hollow organ into which food goes after it is swallowed.

straight (strāt) *adj.* not crooked, curved, etc. [Make a *straight* line.] —**straight' er, straight' est**

strange (strānj) *adj.* different from usual; peculiar; odd [wearing a *strange* costume]. —**strang' er, strang' est** —**strange' ly** *adv.*

stu·di·ous (stoo' dē əs) *adj.* fond of studying [He is a *studious* pupil.] —**stu' di·ous·ly** *adv.*

style (stīl) *n.* the way in which anything is made, done, written, etc. [pointed arches in the Gothic *style*]. —**styled, styl' ing**

sub- (sub, səb) *a prefix meaning* under or below [*Subsoil* is soil under the topsoil.]

sub·ject (sub' jikt) *n.* **1** word or group of words in a sentence about which something is said. **2** a course of study in school.

sub·mis·sion (səb mish' ən) *n.* the act of submitting or giving up; surrender.

sub·mit (səb mit') *v.* to give in to the power of another; surrender [We will never *submit* to the enemy.] —**sub·mit' ted, sub·mit' ting**

sub·scribe (səb skrīb') *v.* to agree to take and pay for [We *subscribed* to the magazine.] —**sub·scribed', sub·scrib' ing** —**sub·scrib' er** *n.*

sub·scrip·tion (səb skrip' shən) *n.* an agreement to take and pay for a magazine, theater tickets, etc.

sub·tract (səb trakt') *v.* to take away [If 3 is *subtracted* from 5, the remainder is 2.]

sub·vert (səb vurt') *v.* to overthrow something established. —**sub·ver·sion** (səb vur' zhən) *n.*

suc·cess (sək ses') *n.* **1** the result that was hoped for; satisfactory outcome [Did you have *success* in training your dog?] **2** the fact of becoming rich, famous, etc. [Her *success* did not change her.]

suc·cess·ful (sək ses' fəl) *adj.* **1** having success; [a *successful* meeting]. **2** having become rich, famous, etc. [a *successful* architect]. —**suc·cess' ful·ly** *adv.*

suf·fix (suf' iks) *n.* a syllable or group of syllables, joined to the end of a word to change its meaning.

sug·ar (shoog' ər) *n.* sweet substances that dissolve in water.

suit·a·ble (soot' ə b'l) *adj.* right for the purpose [a *suitable* gift]. —**suit' a·bil' i·ty** *n.* —**suit' a·bly** *adv.*

sup·ple·ment (sup' lə mənt) *n.* something added [Vitamin pills are a *supplement* to a poor diet.]♦*v.* (sup' lə ment) to add to. —**sup' ple·men' tal** *adj.*

a	fat	ir	here	ou	out	zh	leisure
ā	ape	ī	bite, fire	u	up	ng	ring
ä	car, lot	ō	go	ur	fur		a *in* ago
e	ten	ô	law, horn	ch	chin		e *in* agent
er	care	oi	oil	sh	she	ə	= i *in* unity
ē	even	oo	look	th	thin		o *in* collect
i	hit	ōō	tool	*th*	then		u *in* focus

sup·ply (sə plī′) *v.* to give what is needed [The camp *supplies* sheets and towels.] —**sup·plied′, sup·ply′ ing** ◆*n.* **supplies,** *pl.* things needed; materials [school *supplies*]. —*pl.* **sup·plies′**

sup·port (sə pôrt′) *v.* **1** to carry the weight of [Will that ladder *support* you?] **2** to take the side of; help [He worked to *support* our cause.] —**sup·port′ er** *n.*

sup·pose (sə pōz′) *v.* to expect [It's *supposed* to snow today.] —**sup·posed′, sup·pos′ ing**

sur·face (sur′ fis) *n.* **1** the outside or outer face of a thing [the *surface* of the earth]. **2** any side of a thing having several sides [A box has many *surfaces*.] **3** outward look or features [She was all smiles on the *surface*.] ◆*adj.* of, on, or at the surface [What is the *surface* temperature of the lake?] ◆*v.* to rise to the surface of water. —**sur′ faced, sur′ fac·ing**

surf·board (surf′ bôrd) *n.* a long, narrow board used in surfing.

sur·ger·y (sur′ jər ē) *n.* the treating of disease or injury by operations with the hands or tools. —*pl.* **sur′ ger·ies**

sus·pect (sə spekt′) *v.* to think of as probably guilty [The detective *suspected* the butler of the murder.] ◆*n.* (sus′ pekt) a person suspected of wrongdoing [The stranger was a *suspect* in the robbery.]

sus·pend (sə spend′) *v.* **1** to hang by a support from above [The keys were *suspended* by a chain.] **2** to keep out for a while as a punishment [She was *suspended* from school for misbehaving.] —**sus·pend′ ed, sus·pend′ ing**

syl·la·ble (sil′ ə b'l) *n.* any of the parts into which a written word is divided [The *syllables* of the entry words in this dictionary are divided by tiny dots.]

Syllable comes from a Greek word that means "to put or hold together." Syllables are put together to form words.

sym·pa·thy (sim′ pə thē) *n.* a sharing of feelings [He wept out of *sympathy* for my loss.] —**sym′ pa·thies**

sym·pho·ny (sim′ fə nē) *n.* **1** a long piece of music for a full orchestra. **2** a large orchestra for playing such works. —*pl.* **sym′ pho·nies** —**sym·phon·ic** (sim fän′ ik) *adj.* —**sym·phon′ i·cal·ly** *adv.*

symp·tom (simp′ təm) *n.* sign [Spots on the skin may be a *symptom* of chicken pox.] —**symp·to·mat·ic** (simp′ tə mat′ ik) *adj.*

sys·tem (sis′ təm) *n.* an orderly way of doing things; method [a new *system* for losing weight].

T

take (tāk) *v.* **1** to grasp [*Take* my hand.] **2** to get as one's own [She *took* the job.] **3** to travel by or on [He *took* a bus.] **4** to use up [It *took* all day.] —**took, tak′ en, tak′ ing**

tale (tāl) *n.* **1** a story, especially about things that are made up [The sitter read the children fairy *tales*.] **2** a lie or false story. **3** gossip.

tal·ent (tal′ ənt) *n.* **1** a natural skill that is unusual [She has *talent* as an artist.] **2** people with talent [He helps young *talents* along.]

talk (tôk) *v.* to say words; speak [The baby is learning to *talk*.] —**talk′ er** *n.*

tax (taks) *n.* money one pays to support the government. ◆*v.* **1** to put a tax on [Congress has the power to *tax* the people.] **2** to put a burden or strain on [These pranks *tax* my patience.]

tax·i (tak′ sē) *v.* to move along the ground or water as an airplane does before taking off or landing. —**tax′ ied, tax′ i·ing**

tel·e·graph (tel′ ə graf) *n.* a device or system for sending messages over wire or by radio. ◆*v.* to send by telegraph, as a message.

te·lep·a·thy (tə lep′ ə thē) *n.* the supposed sending of messages from one mind to another, without the help of speech, sight, etc.

tel·e·phone (tel′ ə fōn) *n.* **1** a way of sending sounds over distances. **2** a device for sending and receiving sounds in this way. —**tel·e·phon·ic** (tel′ ə fän′ ik) *adj.*

Telephone comes from two Greek words: *tele*, meaning "far off," and *phone*, meaning "a sound." Alexander G. Bell took the word telephone for his invention in 1876 after the word had been used for other devices.

tel·e·scope (tel′ ə skōp) *n.* a device for making far-off things seem closer. —**tel′ e·scoped, tel′ e·scop·ing**

tel·e·scop·ic (tel′ ə skäp′ ik) *adj.* of a telescope [*telescopic* lens].

tel·e·vi·sion (tel′ ə vizh′ ən) *n.* **1** a way of sending pictures through space by changing the light rays into electric waves which are picked up by a receiver. **2** such a receiver. ◆*adj.* of, using, or sent by television [a *television* program].

tem·po·rar·y (tem′ pə rer′ ē) *adj.* not permanent. —**tem′ po·rar′ i·ly** *adv.*

ten-speed (ten-spēd) *adj.* having ten speeds.

ter·ri·ble (ter′ ə b′l) *adj.* **1** causing great fear. **2** very great; severe [*terrible* suffering]. —**ter′ ri·bly** *adv.*

ter·ri·fy (ter′ ə fī) *v.* to fill with terror; frighten greatly [They were *terrified* by a snake.] —**ter′ ri·fied, ter′ ri·fy·ing**

ter·ror (ter′ ər) *n.* a great fear.

their (*th*er) *adj.* of them or done by them [It is *their* house.]

there's (*th*erz) there is.

ther·mo- (thʉr′ mō) *a combining form meaning* heat.

ther·mom·e·ter (thər mäm′ ə tər) *n.* a device for measuring temperature.

they're (*th*er) they are.

thigh (thī) *n.* the part of the leg between the knee and the hip.

thought·ful (thôt′ fəl) *adj.* **1** showing thought; serious [a *thoughtful* book]. **2** showing care or paying attention to others; considerate [It was *thoughtful* of you to remember her birthday.] —**thought′ ful·ly** *adv.* —**thought′ ful·ness** *n.*

three-fourths (thrē′ fôrths) *adj.* three of the four equal parts of a whole.

thumb (thum) *n.* the short, thick finger nearest the wrist.

to·tal (tōt′ ′l) *n.* the whole amount. —*pl.* **to′ tals** ◆*adj.* entire [The *total* amount of your bill is $3.50.]

to·tal·ly (tōt′ ′l ē) *adv.* completely; entirely.

a	fat	ir	here	ou	out	zh	leisure
ā	ape	ī	bite, fire	u	up	ng	ring
ä	car, lot	ō	go	ʉr	fur		a *in* ago
e	ten	ô	law, horn	ch	chin		e *in* agent
er	care	oi	oil	sh	she	ə =	i *in* unity
ē	even	oo	look	th	thin		o *in* collect
i	hit	o͞o	tool	*th*	then		u *in* focus

train (trān) *v.* **1** to develop the mind, character, etc. of [They *trained* their children to be kind.] **2** to teach, or give practice in, some skill [He can *train* animals to do tricks.] **3** to make or become fit for some sport.

train·ing (trān′ ing) *n.* **1** the practice, drills, etc. given by one who trains or received by one who is being trained. **2** the condition of being trained for some sport.

trai·tor (trāt′ ər) *n.* a person who betrays his or her country, friends, etc.

trai·tor·ous (trāt′ ər əs) *adj.* of or like a traitor or treason; treacherous. —**trai′ tor·ous·ly** *adv.*

trans·mis·sion (trans mish′ ən) *n.* the part of a car that sends the power from the engine to the wheels.

trans·mit (trans mit′) *v.* to send out radio or TV signals. —**trans·mit′ ted, trans·mit′ ting**

trans·por·ta·tion (trans′ pər tā′ shən) *n.* the act of carrying from one place to another.

trav·el (trav′ 'l) *v.* to go from one place to another [He *traveled* around the world.] —**trav′ eled, trav′ el·ing** —**trav′ el·er** *n.*

trick·er·y (trik′ ər ē) *n.* the act of tricking or cheating. —*pl.* **trick′ er·ies**

twen·ty-five (twen′ tē-fīv′) *adj.* the number 25.

twi·light (twī′ līt) *n.* the time between sunset and dark.

type (tīp) *v.* to write with a typewriter. —**typed, typ′ ing**

type·writer (tīp′ rīt′ ər) *n.* a machine for making printed letters on paper.

ty·phoon (tī foon′) *n.* any violent tropical cyclone that starts in the western Pacific.

typ·i·cal (tip′ i k'l) *adj.* characteristic [The snail moved with *typical* slowness.] —**typ′ i·cal·ly** *adv.*

ty·rant (tī′ rənt) *n.* **1** a ruler having complete power. **2** a person who uses power in a cruel way [Your boss is a *tyrant.*]

U

un- (un, ən) **1** *a prefix meaning* not *or* the opposite of [An *unhappy* person is one who is not happy, but sad.] **2** *a prefix meaning* to reverse or undo the action of [To *untie* a shoelace is to reverse the action of tying it.]

un·com·mon (un käm′ ən) *adj.* rare; unusual. —**un·com′ mon·ly** *adv.*

un·e·qual (un ē′ kwəl) *adj.* not equal, as in amount, size, strength, value, or rank. [We were given *unequal* shares.] —**un·e′ qual·ly** *adv.*

un·i·den·ti·fied (un′ ī den′ tə fīd) *adj.* not identified; not known or recognized.

u·nite (yoo nīt′) *v.* to join together to make one; combine [The two churches *united* to form a new church.] —**u·nit′ ed, u·nit′ ing**

un·named (un nāmd′) *adj.* not named or identified.

un·nec·es·sar·y (un nes′ ə ser′ ē) *adj.* not necessary; needless [an *unnecessary* argument]. —**un·nec′ es·sar′ i·ly** *adv.*

un·nerve (un nʉrv′) *v.* to make lose nerve, courage, or control [The accident *unnerved* him.] —**un·nerved′, un·nerv′ ing**

un·num·bered (un num′ bərd) *adj.* not numbered or counted.

un·re·al (un rē′ əl *or* un rēl′) *adj.* not real; imaginary or made up. —**un·re·al·i·ty** (un′ rē al′ ə tē) *n.*

un·suc·cess·ful (un′ sək ses′ fəl) *adj.* not successful. —**un′ suc·cess′ ful·ly** *adv.*

un·veil (un vāl′) *v.* to take a veil or covering from so as to reveal [*Unveil* the statue.] —**un·veil·ing** (un vāl′ ing) *n.* a formal or ceremonial removal of a covering from a statue, etc.

us·a·ble (yo͞o′ zə b′l) *adj.* that can be used; fit or ready for use.

V

var·i·ous (ver′ ē əs) *adj.* of several different kinds [We planted *various* seeds.] —**var′ i·ous·ly** *adv.*

veil (vāl) *n.* a piece of thin cloth worn by women over the face or head [a bride's *veil*; a nun's *veil*]. ◆*v.* to cover, hide, etc. with a veil.

vein (vān) *n.* any blood vessel that carries blood back to the heart.

ver·dict (vʉr′ dikt) *n.* the decision reached by a jury in a law case [a *verdict* of "not guilty"].

ver·sion (vʉr′ zhən) *n.* a report from one's point of view [Give us your *version* of the accident.]

vic·to·ri·ous (vik tôr′ ē əs) *adj.* winning or conquering.

vig·or (vig′ ər) *n.* strength and energy of the body or mind [He walked with vigor.]

vig·or·ous (vig′ ər əs) *adj.* full of vigor or energy [He is a *vigorous* public official.] —**vig′ or·ous·ly** *adv.*

vil·lain (vil′ ən) *n.* an evil or wicked person, or such a character in a play, novel, etc.

vil·lain·ous (vil′ ən əs) *adj.* evil; wicked [He writes *villainous* plots.] —**vil′ lain·ous·ly** *adv.*

vin·e·gar (vin′ i gər) *n.* a sour liquid made by fermenting cider, wine, malt, etc.

vis·i·tor (viz′ it ər) *n.* a person making a visit; guest.

vo·cab·u·lar·y (vō kab′ yə ler′ ē) *n.* a list of words, usually alphabetical, as in a dictionary. —*pl.* **vo·cab′ u·lar′ ies**

W

walk (wôk) *v.* to move on foot at a normal speed [*Walk*, do not run, to the nearest exit.]

wal·rus (wôl′ rəs *or* wäl′ rus) *n.* a large sea animal like the seal, found in northern oceans.

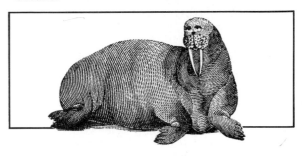

waltz (wôlts *or* wôls) *n.* a dance with three beats to the measure. ◆*v.* to dance a waltz.

wash·a·ble (wôsh′ ə b′l) *adj.* that can be washed without being damaged.

wear·a·ble (wer′ ə b′l) *adj.* that can be worn.

weight (wāt) *n.* amount of heaviness [What is your *weight*?]

weird (wird) *adj.* very odd, strange, etc. [a *weird* hat]. —**weird′ ly** *adv.* —**weird′ ness** *n.*

Weird comes to us from an old English word meaning "fate." The earliest meaning of *weird* is that of "having to do with fate or destiny." When we don't understand why certain things happen, they seem mysterious, brought about by fate.

a	fat	ir	here	ou	out	zh	leisure
ā	ape	ī	bite, fire	u	up	ng	ring
ä	car, lot	ō	go	ʉr	fur		a *in* ago
e	ten	ô	law, horn	ch	chin		e *in* agent
er	care	oi	oil	sh	she	ə = i *in* unity
ē	even	oo	look	th	thin		o *in* collect
i	hit	o͞o	tool	*th*	then		u *in* focus

well-bal·anced (wel′ bal′ ənst) *adj.* having the needed parts in the right amounts [a *well-balanced* meal].

whole (hōl) *adj.* not divided; in one piece [Put *whole* carrots in the stew.]
—**whole′ ness** *n.*

whole-sale (hōl′ sāl) *n.* the sale of goods in large amounts, especially to retail stores. ◆*adj.* having to do with such a sale of goods [a *wholesale* dealer]. ◆*adv.* in wholesale amounts or at wholesale prices [We are buying the clothes *wholesale*.]
—**whole′ sal·er** *n.*

who's (hōōz) who is.

worse (wʉrs) *adj.* more evil, harmful, bad, etc.

would've (wood′ əv) would have.

wrench (rench) *n.* a tool for holding and turning nuts, bolts, pipes, etc.

wrist (rist) *n.* the joint between the hand and forearm.

wrist·watch (rist′ wäch) *n.* a watch worn on a strap or band that fits around the wrist. —*pl.* **wrist′ watch·es**

writ·er (rīt′ ər) *n.* a person whose work is writing books, articles, etc.; author.

Y

yacht (yät) *n.* a large boat or small ship for racing, taking pleasure cruises, etc.

you're (yoor) you are.

a	fat	ir	here	ou	out	zh	leisure
ā	ape	ī	bite, fire	u	up	ng	ring
ä	car, lot	ō	go	ʉr	fur		a *in* ago
e	ten	ô	law, horn	ch	chin		e *in* agent
er	care	oi	oil	sh	she	ə =	i *in* unity
ē	even	oo	look	th	thin		o *in* collect
i	hit	ōō	tool	th	then		u *in* focus

Handwriting Practice

Lesson **2**

laughable

movable

Lesson **4**

rearrange

reinvest

Lesson **5**

reflect

detect

Lesson **6**

addresses

waltzes

Lesson **7**

magazine

gigantic

Lesson **10**

enjoys

activities

Lesson 11

originally

equally

Lesson 12

mountainous

joyous

Lesson 13

unnumbered

misjudge

Lesson 14

explore

subject

Lesson 15

grocery

slavery

Lesson 16

chrome

rhythm

Lesson 19

patrolled

omitted

Lesson 20

library

February

Lesson 21

freight

vein

Lesson 22

community

combat

Lesson 23

adjective

assignment

Lesson 24

regular

burglar

Lesson 25

thumb

doubt

Lesson 28

geography

microscope

Lesson 29

they're

three-fourths

Lesson 30

inventor

mirror

Lesson 31

exaggerate

exhibit

Lesson 32

impolite

appointment

Lesson 34

campaign

thoughtful